SEMINAR EDITIONS

SEMINAR EDITIONS

Theodore G. Tappert, General Editor

THE JOURNALS
OF ERIC NORELIUS

A SWEDISH MISSIONARY
ON THE AMERICAN FRONTIER

Translated, edited, and with an Introduction by

G. EVERETT ARDEN

FORTRESS PRESS • PHILADELPHIA

SEMINAR EDITIONS

Christian literature of the past, when read and pondered after the lapse of generations, often sheds new light on the discussion of important questions in our day. Revival of interest in the writings of such diverse figures of the past as Søren Kierkegaard, Blaise Pascal, John Wesley, John Calvin, Martin Luther, Thomas Aquinas, and Augustine (to mention only a few) has served such a function.

Acquaintance with the literature of the past also provides first-hand glimpses into the life and thought of Christians in earlier ages. Men whose names have been encountered in history textbooks take on flesh and blood, and important movements in the history of the church come into clearer focus when the literary deposit of other times is read.

It is the purpose of the present series to make available to the modern reader a number of works which deserve to be better known. Most of them are here translated into English for the first time; the few which were originally written in English have long been out of print. All have been edited with care and furnished with introductions and annotations which will help the reader understand them in their historical context.

The choice of various types of literature—diaries, memoirs, and correspondence as well as theological essays—should add interest to instruction for the general reader as well as the student of church history and the history of Christian thought. The same may be said for the inclusion of European as well as American works.

CONTENTS

Introduction, by G. Everett Arden   1

The Text of the *Journals*   39

1   Early Years and Emigration (1833-1851)   41

2   Student at Capital University (1851-1853)   78

3   Interim of Work and Travel (1853-1854)   116

4   Minister to Immigrants (1855-1856)   142

5   Missionary Journey to the West Coast (1885-1886)   156

Index   201

INTRODUCTION

G. Everett Arden

The Immigrant

The story of Eric Norelius is not merely the story of one man; it is really the story of a people, a church, and a Christian ministry which was in many respects fairly typical of the American frontier of the nineteenth century. What he was, what he hoped for, what he endured, and what he achieved may be said to symbolize the sacrifices, aspirations, and accomplishments of a whole generation of pioneers who wrested from the harsh American wilderness the abundant life which the Old World could not offer.

Norelius came to America as a typical immigrant. He was a part of that vast tidal wave of humanity, drawn from all parts of the world, which swarmed to these shores during the greater part of the nineteenth century in search of freedom and opportunity. Like the majority of his counterparts, he had left his native land to come to America, not out of religious motivations, but chiefly for economic reasons. His homeland, Sweden, like many other European countries, was undergoing a vast transformation from a rural and agrarian to an urban and industrial social order.[1] Such pro-

[1] See G. Everett Arden, *The School of the Prophets* (Rock Island, Ill.: Augustana Book Concern, 1960), chaps. 1-4, pp. 3-57. Eli Heckscher, *Svenskt arbete och liv* (Stockholm: Svenska kyrkans diakonistyrelses bokförlag, 1942), chap. 5, pp. 167-272, and chap. 6, pp. 273-336. A. A. Stomberg, *A History of Sweden* (New York: Macmillan, 1931), chaps. 23 and 24, pp. 616-679. *Emigrationsutredningen*, a definitive study of immigration and emigration in

1

found changes not only brought new and better opportunities for thousands who were trained and equipped to take advantage of the new situation, but at the same time created severe dislocations and hardships for thousands of others less fortunate. For these immigration seemed to offer an attractive solution to their problems.

As the son of a small farmer in north-central Sweden, Eric Norelius faced a rather limited future at home. The most natural course for him would have been to follow in the footsteps of his father and upon reaching manhood to rent a few acres of stony ground from which to eke out a meager livelihood. But even this would have been difficult, since the productive land was gradually coming under the control of wealthy landowners, while the poorer agricultural classes were finding it increasingly difficult to acquire tenant rights even to marginal land.[2] To a boy with a lively imagination, a strong will, and a good deal of stubborn determination, this was a bleak and uncertain prospect. Could he not acquire an education and by this means lift himself into a more promising future, perhaps even into the ministry of the church? But an education cost money, and here was the rub. The solution to this economic problem was suggested to young Eric by a neighboring minister, Anders Wiberg of Söderhamm, who advised the young man to go to America, where "it would doubtless be easier for a penniless student to receive an education . . . than in Sweden."[3] Just as the promise of cheap land on the American fron-

Sweden, published by the Swedish government between 1908 and 1913, and comprising 21 volumes, states that Swedish immigration to the U. S. A. between 1860 and 1910 totaled 933,958, including 523,920 men and 410,038 women. Bilaga XX, p. 114, table 14.

[2] The area of cultivated land in Sweden increased more than threefold from 1750 to 1850, but the increase in population, especially among the poorer agricultural classes, was even greater. By the middle of the nineteenth century the landless agricultural population could no longer find sufficient employment in farming to insure an adequate standard of living. *Emigrationsutredningen,* Bilaga VIII, p. 7. John Lindberg, *Background of Swedish Emigration* (Minneapolis: University of Minnesota Press, 1930), pp. 109 ff. A. A. Stomberg, *op. cit.,* pp. 637 ff.

[3] *Journals,* p. 48 below. The appeal which emigration had for the landless agricultural population in Sweden is reflected by the fact that in the period

tier with the prospect of eventual prosperity and economic security induced countless thousands of Europeans to forsake home and kindred in the Old World and cast their lot amidst the perils and hardships of the New World, so the hope for a cheap education with its eventual emoluments beckoned to Eric Norelius with irresistible allure.

To cross the Atlantic Ocean a hundred years ago was no small undertaking. It required a good deal of nerve and determination to face the prospect of a perilous and uncomfortable sea voyage which, if it was successful, might very well last for two or even three months. There was need, too, for strong bodies, robust health, and hardy constitutions, for the long and dreary weeks at sea invariably involved exposure to contagious diseases and contaminated food and water. Passenger quarters were often terribly overcrowded and included only the most primitive facilities for the preparation of food and personal sanitation. On most ships carrying immigrants the passengers were not only required to furnish their own bedding and food supplies, but also had to prepare and serve their own food, using the galley facilities of the ship as opportunity afforded. There was, of course, no medical doctor on the staff of an average immigrant ship, and in case of sickness or accident each family was expected to care for its own as it was able.

It was after such a sea voyage, which Norelius tells us lasted for seventy-five days, that young Eric arrived in New York Harbor aboard the little schooner "Odin," on Thursday, October 31, 1850. With a fine sense of restraint he recorded his first impressions regarding this bewildering experience. "We were deeply impressed," he wrote, "as we surveyed the broad scene of the great city and its environs."[4]

1850-1860, 15,184 immigrants from the rural population landed in America, in contrast to 1,711 drawn from urban districts. From 1861 to 1870, 45,400 agricultural workers in contrast to 18,700 industrial workers came from Sweden to the United States. For statistics see *Emigrationsutredningen*, Bilaga V, table 6.

[4] *Journals*, p. 55 below.

Impressive though it was, New York was merely a stopover along the way toward Eric's ultimate destination in America. Far out west on the American frontier was a place called Andover, in Henry County, Illinois. This was the ultimate destination of Norelius and his friends. But between New York and Andover there stretched a perilous, tedious, and expensive inland journey equal in extent to the entire length of faraway Sweden. Why not settle in New York or in some other nearby place where a young man able and willing to work hard might well find suitable opportunities for advancement in America? Why endure the unknown hardships of a thousand-mile trek into America's "wilderness land"?

In steering his course toward Andover, Illinois, Norelius was simply doing what practically all other immigrants found it both expedient and necessary to do, namely, to identify himself closely and intimately with his own national group in this new land, wherever such a group existed. It was to Andover that the Rev. Lars Paul Esbjörn, a clergyman of the Church of Sweden, had led a large immigrant party in 1849, and there established a Swedish Lutheran congregation. Esbjörn was the first clergyman from the Church of Sweden to cast his lot with the Swedish immigrants of the nineteenth century, coming to America to minister to his countrymen here. His departure from Sweden and subsequent reports of his American mission published in several Swedish newspapers were headline news and served to make his name and his work known throughout the Swedish realm. The little Swedish Lutheran community in Andover thus became the fixed point in the compass of countless Swedish immigrants who instinctively felt that if they could only manage to reach Andover, most of their troubles would be over and their problems solved. It was this naïve sentiment which impelled Norelius to set his sights toward Andover, not counting the cost. To him Andover appeared like a haven in an alien world; there he would find help among his own people; there he would find his own niche.

To be able to identify himself with a community of his own nationality in America was a tremendous boon to the early immigrant. Such identification was practically the only promise of security which the newcomer possessed in the midst of a pluralistic and highly competitive society. Unless he had unusual resources of his own, the average immigrant was happy indeed to take advantage of both the temporal and spiritual resources which might be available to him within the context of the community, for here he met familiar conditions in unfamiliar surroundings. The community provided the framework within which the heritage of values, traditions, and customs was expressed and preserved, giving continuity and meaning to the life and future of the transplanted newcomer. The community shielded him from the vagaries of predatory forces. Within the community the immigrant would be most likely to find the doors of opportunity opening for him. For such reasons the stream of immigration coming to America tended to separate at the ports of debarkation into national groups, each of them seeking out those communities in the New World to which they were kindred.

Although the national community was in so many ways a boon to the immigrant, it was not entirely an unmitigated blessing. Precisely because it provided a haven in a new and bewildering environment, shielding the newcomer from unfriendly forces, repristinating his European heritage, especially his language and religion, and thereby emphasizing the elements of differentiation and discontinuity in the immigrant's relationship to the New World, it tended to isolate him from the broader American community. The embrace of the national community tended to foster and deepen in the immigrant a firm loyalty to his European heritage. This loyalty often expressed itself, not only in renewed positive commitment, but also negatively in suspicion and withdrawal from all who differed from the group. This tended to alienate the immigrant from the more inclusive structures of his neighborhood, making his adjustment to the American environment both more difficult and more tardy than it otherwise might have been.

Eric Norelius is a typical example of this immigrant loyalty and its consequent exclusiveness. On his journey toward Andover, Norelius had two opportunities to chart a relatively easy course toward security for himself. The first was in New York, when in consultation with the Swedish Methodist missionary, Olof G. Hedstrom, he had been invited to forsake his Lutheran heritage and join the Methodist church in exchange for the vague promise of financial aid toward an education.[5] The second opportunity came in Chicago when the Swedish Episcopal missionary, Gustaf Unonius, beckoned in the same direction.[6] But since the chances for a successful realization of his dreams seemed to lie not in the vague and uncertain promises given by strangers, but rather with the community in Andover with which he felt more nearly kindred, he refused to be diverted from the course he had set for himself.

Having finally arrived in Andover he found the Rev. Mr. Esbjörn to be "a kind, sympathetic, scholarly and perhaps somewhat stubborn person, who had a real love for his flock," and whose opinion and advice were more nearly in agreement with Eric's own ideas than any other person he had consulted. Indeed, the first real home young Eric had in America was in the Esbjörn household, where he stayed from the time of his arrival in Andover, in November, until the middle of December, 1850.[7] This marked the beginning of an intimate friendship between Esbjörn and Norelius which was to last for life. Each became the confidant and firm supporter of the other.

But of even greater significance is the fact that this marked the beginning of Norelius' life-long identification with that community which Esbjörn originally headed and which ultimately became the

[5] *Journals,* entry for October 31, 1850.
[6] *Journals,* entry for November 16, 1850.
[7] *Journals,* p. 67 below.

Augustana Lutheran Church. Norelius served this community for over sixty years as pastor, editor, missionary, and twice as its president. It was out of loyalty to this community that he declined to separate from the Augustana Synod and form an independent Minnesota Synod in 1858, in spite of his own ambitions and inclinations and heavy pressure from a number of his Minnesota colleagues.[8]

Fidelity to his community, however, was not the only form which Norelius' loyalty took. He was also suspicious of those who seemed to differ with the viewpoint and practices to which he and his national group were committed, and he seemed anxious to withdraw from all such associations. Time and again in the *Journals* he voices his disapproval of the theology and the religious climate which prevailed at Capital University in Columbus. The sermons and lectures to which he listened often seemed shallow and even Pelagian, while the conduct of many of his fellow students appeared to be frivolous and unseemly. Thus, before the end of his first semester at Columbus, he was giving serious thought to dropping out of school and continuing his education by private study.[9] Again, when his friends Anders Wiberg and Gustaf Palmquist renounced their Lutheran heritage and became Baptists, Norelius parted company with them and bemoaned their unfaithfulness.[10]

Later in the spring of 1853, Norelius received a letter from his family in Sweden informing him that they were following his example and were pulling up stakes in the old homeland and coming to America. Norelius was dumfounded and expressed his dis-

---

[8] Commenting on this situation in his *De Svenska Luterska Församlingarnas och Svenskarnes Historia i Amerika,* Vol. I (Rock Island, Ill.: Lutheran Augustana Book Concern, 1890), p. 848, Norelius declares: ". . . who can wonder that . . . both pastors and congregations in Minnesota were disgruntled and desired a change [i.e., the establishment of an independent Minnesota Synod]. . . . What deterred us was quite simply our national loyalty."

[9] *Journals,* entries for December 1 and 5, 1851.

[10] *Journals,* entry for July 14, 1852.

may in an outburst of emotion. "This means," he wrote, "that I shall never again see my native land, never have the opportunity of living and working there as I had hoped. . . . Must I now behold the eventual loss of a genuine and noble Swedish heritage as it becomes mingled and eventually absorbed by an American culture? . . . As for myself, I shall struggle against this danger."[11]

This is, to be sure, the cry of a lonely and bewildered nineteen-year-old youth bitterly bewailing the loss of a cherished dream and ambition. He had looked forward to the day when he could return to the old homeland and take his place among his former friends and acquaintances, not as a lowly tenant farmer now, but as an educated man of importance and distinction, a leader in his community. And now this hope seemed to be shattered. But more than that, he had developed a new and deeper appreciation for his Swedish religious and cultural heritage and feared the adulteration which he was sure would result from continued contact with the American environment.

This same spirit of exclusiveness is not entirely lacking in Norelius' later life and ministry. When, for example, L. P. Esbjörn abruptly resigned from the theological faculty of the fledgling Lutheran seminary at Springfield, Illinois, and proposed, on both nationalistic and theological grounds, to sever all connections with the Synod of Northern Illinois and to organize an independent Scandinavian Lutheran Synod, he turned first to Norelius for encouragement and support, for he knew that Norelius was sympathetic with a more exclusive Scandinavian Lutheranism in America.[12] To this appeal Norelius responded both positively and energetically, defending Esbjörn's actions by both the spoken and the written word and by his participation in the establishment of the

---

[11] *Journals,* entry for May 7, 1853.

[12] An account of the Springfield rupture is given in G. Everett Arden, *The School of the Prophets,* pp. 87 ff. See also George M. Stephenson, *The Founding of the Augustana Synod* (Rock Island, Ill.: Augustana Book Concern, 1927), chaps. 1-3.

Augustana Synod at Jefferson Prairie, Wisconsin, in June, 1860. Again, in 1911, Robert H. Gardiner of Boston, Massachusetts, secretary of the Episcopal Commission on Faith and Order, sent Norelius, who was then president of the Augustana Synod, an invitation to participate in a World Conference on Faith and Order, and to this ecumenical overture Norelius sent a rather curt reply, saying in effect that neither he nor his synod was interested in any talk about unity which cut across denominational lines.[13]

In the exclusiveness of Norelius we can detect the blending of both cultural and confessional loyalties. These loyalties seemed equally necessary because both seemed to be mutually supporting in an age when little or no thought was given to ecumenical relationships. Sectarian emphases were considered to be indispensable to survival in the prevailing fierce competition between, and even within, denominations.

To Norelius, as to most discerning immigrant leaders, acculturation appeared inevitable but dangerous, for it threatened to erode and vitiate those values which were peculiarly distinctive of the national group. It was such distinguishing values that gave cohesion to the immigrant community, holding it together and therefore providing a practical synthesis of cultural and confessional values for immigrant life in the new American environment. This was especially important for the work of the church, because emigration from home and family all too often included abandonment of former ties with religion and church.[14] The differentiated community therefore had a dual role to play in the missionary program of the church. In the first place, it had to be the evangelizing agency which would provide the resources of men and means

[13] The full text of the Gardiner-Norelius correspondence is given in *Referat*, Augustana Synod, 1911, pp. 36 f.

[14] In 1870 there were approximately 97,000 Swedish nationals in the United States. Of this number, the largest Swedish-American institution in America, the Augustana Synod, had succeeded in winning to its membership only a little more than 19,000. See G. Everett Arden, *Augustana Heritage* (Rock Island, Ill.: Augustana Press, 1963), p. 15.

for reaching the widely scattered immigrants and incorporating them into a new church home in their new homeland. In the second place, it also had to constitute a precinct with a sufficient pattern of familiarity to be attractive to an uprooted folk seeking to establish new foundations. As long as the immigrant would constitute the major missionary concern of the church on the frontier, so long would it be imperative to maintain a distinctive and differentiated community in which the blending of both cultural and confessional loyalties obtained.

It was recognized and acknowledged by Norelius and other pioneer leaders, however, that in a later day when the new settlers had become old settlers, and a new generation had emerged which had been born, reared, and educated in America, the need for a culturally, nationalistically differentiated community would no longer be an imperative need. While confessional fidelity to the unchanging Word of God must ever prevail, the mode and means through which such witness is articulated would have to be adapted to the changing times.[15]

The New Settler

The American dream of a better and brighter future which beguiled so many hundreds of thousands of people, persuading them to forsake homeland and kindred in Europe and turn their faces toward the great open country of the American West, was not an illusion. For most of them their dreams came true, their hopes were realized, in some cases beyond the wildest stretch of the imagination. Those who failed were the exceptions, even though they may have been many. The cost of success and failure alike, however, ran high, for the pathway of the new settler, whatever

[15] For example, the concern which Norelius felt for making the ministry of the church relevant to the youth through the use of the English language is expressed in numerous references scattered through his reports to both the Minnesota Conference and the Augustana Synod.

the eventual outcome of his endeavor, invariably led through the valley of trial and tribulation. The pioneer days, which seem so romantic when viewed from the long perspective of a century or more, were in reality a time of suffering, deprivation, and hardship. There were very few cheap victories; most of the achievements of the new settlers were purchased with "blood, sweat, and tears."

As a pioneer in the American midwest, Eric Norelius shared in the hardships and trials of those who won the west for future generations. His experiences were in no sense unique or unusual but may be said to have been rather typical of the average new settler in midwestern America during the early decades of the nineteenth century. The fact that he became a pastor did not mitigate his hardships or exempt him from suffering and adversity. On the contrary, it may well have increased his troubles, since the pressures of pastoral duties and responsibilities permitted him to give only a minimum of attention to his own personal, temporal affairs. As a pioneer minister he was called on to sacrifice health, strength, time, and economic welfare for the sake of his ministry. Indeed, from the very beginning of his American pilgrimage Eric Norelius traveled the same rough road of personal sacrifice which was the common lot of most new settlers.

There were, for example, the difficulties and hardships attendant upon travel and transportation. The newcomer who arrived in this country during the first half of the last century found the settled East a difficult place to gain a foothold in the New World, and therefore the mainstream of immigration pushed its way over the Allegheny Mountains toward the free land of the western frontier. But to reach the frontier meant a long and rigorous journey.

The usual route inland from New York to Chicago was by steamer up the Hudson River to Albany, then by boat through the Eire Canal to Buffalo, on to Cleveland, and through the Great Lakes to Chicago. From Chicago there were boat routes leading to the Mississippi and wagon trails fanning out westward across the rolling prairies.

The enterprising promoters who owned and operated the various transportation facilities leading westward were in business for the sake of profit, and there were no regulating agencies to supervise or control the methods by which they made their profits. There were no rules governing the number of people who could be carried at any one time, nor minimum standards of safety, comfort, or sanitation. The result was that in many cases the immigrants were bilked, defrauded, and swindled as they exchanged their European money for American dollars, bought tickets for their journey, or arranged for the transport of their baggage. Often they were treated more like cattle than human beings, crowded into ships, railroad cars, and canal boats by twice or even three times the number for which accommodations were intended. The boat which carried Norelius from Buffalo to Chicago, the S. S. "Sultana," is described in the *Journals* as "a wretched, ramshackle, old hulk without comforts or conveniences,"[16] and when Norelius speaks of the canal boat which took him from Chicago to La Salle, Illinois, he reports that the boat "was overcrowded and had no conveniences; indeed, there was not even enough room for the passengers to lie down to sleep."[17]

Crowded and unsanitary living conditions, tainted food and water, and the physical debilitation brought on by exposure and fatigue laid the traveling immigrant open to illness and contagious disease, particularly the dreaded cholera and typhoid. Few if any immigrant parties traveling over extended distances escaped a siege of disease and death. Immigrant records are filled with pathetic accounts of families losing father, mother, or children and of stopping only long enough to give the loved one a quick burial in a shallow grave in a sand bank along the way; of entire families

[16] Entry for November 8, 1850.
[17] Entry for November 16, 1850.

swept away in a few days; or of parents losing their lives and leaving their little children to be cared for by others who had enough problems and troubles of their own. The frequent references in his *Journals* to such occurrences testify to the many times Norelius witnessed similar tragedies during the course of his journey from Sweden to Andover.[18]

When there were no other available means of transportation the immigrants walked. To a twentieth-century generation accustomed to the train, the automobile, and the airplane, it seems incredible that the early settlers would strike out across open country, often accompanied by small children and aged folk, walking long distances in all kinds of weather. In one of the most dramatic scenes in the *Journals* Norelius describes a trek by foot across sixty-five miles of open prairie in late November when the bite of winter was in the air. Three days later Norelius and his companions straggled into Andover in the midst of a snowstorm, only to find that even here there was little room for strangers.[19]

In addition to the physical discomforts of frontier life as exemplified by the lack of decent transportation facilities, there was also the grinding poverty so often characteristic of pioneer life. The immigrants who came to America, especially prior to the period of the Civil War, were generally not entirely destitute, since by the economic standards of that day it required a fairly substantial outlay of cash to make the trip to the new West. Those who belonged to the very lowest economic classes in Europe usually found it impossible to raise the necessary capital to make the break from home. It must be conceded, however, that the average immigrant had very meager resources.[20]

---

[18] Cf. entries for August 24, September 21, October 20, 22, and 31, and November 16, 1850.

[19] *Journals,* entries for November 20-23, 1850.

[20] After the Civil War, the rise of a great industrial complex in the United States witnessed the importation of cheap labor forces, at company expense, by the great corporations; many of these workers came from economically depressed areas in Europe.

So far as the Swedish immigrant is concerned, about one in ten had been a small farmer who had sold out his modest holdings and with this money hoped to gain a foothold in America. The vast majority, however, were the sons or sons-in-law of small farmers, who because of restrictive inheritance laws or other complicating factors had come to feel that it was impossible to secure a favorable economic future in the homeland. Therefore, they had determined to make a new start in the New World, hoping that by hard work and patient endurance of hardship and sacrifice they might ultimately provide a better future for themselves and their families. Some of these young men, who had owned no land themselves, had accumulated sufficient funds from gifts, inheritances, and loans to pay for the ocean voyage as well as provide a small surplus to make a start in America. Others had just about enough for the ocean passage and very little more, trusting in some sort of miracle to see them through the hard pioneer period.[21]

Eric Norelius undoubtedly belonged to the latter class. He tells us in the *Journals* that the fare to America for himself and his brother amounted to three hundred rix-dollars, the entire cost of which was assumed by his "indefatigable and faithful father." According to his own testimony, young Norelius was practically destitute when he arrived in Andover and therefore had to begin immediately to look for work. The *Journals* graphically describe the frustrating difficulties which Norelius and his friends encountered as they sought employment in Illinois. Indeed, for the first few months in America Norelius was compelled to accept charity from others who, though poor themselves, generously offered him bed and board until he could find gainful employment. Meanwhile the Rev. Mr. Esbjörn arranged for Eric's enrollment at Capital University in Columbus, Ohio, as a charity student. Although he worked at a number of odd jobs during his stay in Columbus, he was not

[21] *Emigrationsutredningen,* Bilaga VII, pp. 8 f. See also Arden, *School of the Prophets,* pp. 8 ff.

able to earn enough even to keep himself in clothes but had to accept the castoff garments of others while he received aid for board and room.

After he had left school and become a pastor, ministering to his scattered countrymen, poverty continued to plague Norelius for many years. Most of the people to whom he came were poor in earthly possessions and were struggling to make ends meet. They were therefore unable to pay the pastor an adequate wage. Indeed, when Norelius moved to Red Wing, Minnesota, he and his eighteen-year-old wife faced a very uncertain future.

The general poverty among the early settlers on the frontier exacted a terrible toll of sickness and death. Medical help was almost nonexistent in the scattered settlements, and the simple home remedies used by the average family were of little avail against outbreaks of the dreaded cholera, smallpox, and typhoid. When an epidemic would break out there was little that could be done except to keep vigil at the bedside of the stricken one while the disease ran its course, and all too often the culmination was death. Indeed, in times of severe epidemics deaths in a community would be so frequent and numerous that the victims were buried in mass graves because there was neither time nor strength to provide separate graves for the many who succumbed. The mortality rate in childbirth was high for both mother and offspring, and the odds for a child's survival during the first five years of life were not favorable.

Among both old and young the incidence of tuberculosis was high. Norelius makes frequent mention of his own severe and prolonged respiratory troubles, and on several occasions he was compelled to retire from active work for extended periods in order to recover his health. It is not unlikely that at various times in his life he was battling an active case of tuberculosis.

Pioneer hardship was not limited to physical suffering; there were also other more subtle tribulations which burden the mind and spirit. To be isolated and lonely, bereft of those human associations which revivify and lift the soul, is a kind of suffering as real and tormenting as any physical discomfort. Records of the early pioneer period, including Norelius' *Journals,* are full of references to the loneliness and the sense of isolation which depressed those who were struggling to find a place for themselves in a new and sometimes harsh and cruel environment. To be sure, those who settled in the populated sections did not suffer the loss of a sense of community felt by those who settled in the hinterland areas. But it was in the hinterland, in the unsettled wilderness country, that cheap land was to be had for the asking, and it was therefore to these isolated areas that the greater number of newcomers made their way. In these remote places there was still room for a man to find a homestead and grab a stake for himself in the New World.

It is doubtful if there was any trouble more perplexing and distracting for both pastors and people than the quarrels and bickerings which so often occurred in connection with denominational competition. The pioneer period had no comity arrangements among churches, and each denomination felt free to poach on the precincts of another, proselyting wherever possible and gaining advantage over rival groups by whatever means the laws of the land and the restrictions of conscience allowed. Eric Norelius and his colaborers had their full share of trouble with the Baptists, Methodists, and the Episcopalians, all of whom sought to establish missionary programs among the Swedish settlers in order to draw them away from the Lutheran faith and into their own camp.

Religious strife did not always originate from other denominations. On occasion it could and did arise from within the community itself. Beginning about 1876, the Augustana Lutheran Synod, which Norelius loved and served so faithfully, was torn and shaken by the most serious doctrinal crisis in its history, namely, the Waldenstrom controversy. The issue, involving a novel interpretation of the doctrine of the atonement, had first been raised in Sweden by the Rev. P. P. Waldenstrom, a popular preacher and member of the Church of Sweden. Waldenstrom was well known throughout Scandinavia and had many ardent admirers in America. Soon the questions he had raised in Sweden became burning issues in this country, especially among Swedish immigrants. Eric Norelius was president of the Augustana Synod at the time of the outbreak of this acrimonious dispute. It was therefore his responsibility to lead the action against the Waldenstrom factions. It was Norelius who presided at the heresy trial of the Rev. J. G. Princell, chief spokesman for the views of Waldenstrom and pastor of the Gustavus Adolphus congregation in New York City. It was Norelius who, as the synod's chief administrative officer, had to seek to maintain the integrity of both doctrine and practice within the synod. It was under his administration that the synod suffered the most severe rupture in its history as hundreds of members, a number of congregations, and several of the synod's pastors severed their connections with the Augustana Synod and joined the Mission Covenant Church in America.[22]

The Churchman

Most of the Scandinavians who settled in the Mississippi Valley during the nineteenth century were Lutherans, but they were nevertheless a diverse lot. There was a good deal of difference, for example, between a churchman like J. W. C. Dietrichson, the Norwegian evangelist who sought to repristinate the Church of Norway with its emphasis upon ecclesiastical order and discipline, and T. N. Hasselquist, the Swede who favored a freer church order and often entered his pulpit dressed in a sack coat. In spite of such apparent diversities, however, the vast majority of Scandinavian settlers were Lutherans who had been reared and confirmed in the

[22] For an account of the Waldenstrom controversy see Arden, *Augustana Heritage,* chap. 9, pp. 160 ff.

Lutheran church of their homelands and had subsequently felt the influence of the great evangelical revivals that swept through all the Scandinavian lands during the first half of the nineteenth century.

Eric Norelius was such a Lutheran. In his loyalty to the historic confessions of his church as well as his insistence upon experiential religion, he may be thought of as a representative Scandinavian Lutheran and churchman in the early days of midwest Lutheranism.

Like most of his contemporaries in America, Norelius was not a profound thinker; he did not conceive of religion as a set of systematic formulations, nor did he even take time to set forth his own religious views in schematized form. His theology is reflected, however, in his writings.

He came from a deeply religious parental home where regular church attendance, Bible reading, and prayer were a vital part of family life. When the evangelical revivals swept through Scandinavia, it was in such pious family circles that the impact and influence of this movement were most deeply felt. The religious emphases stemming from the revivalists Frederick Gabriel Hedberg, of Finland, and Carl Olof Rosenius, of Sweden, were particularly decisive in the experience of Norelius.

Though Hedberg and Rosenius had their personal as well as theological differences, they were agreed that Christianity is fundamentally the proclamation of the good news of forgiveness, life, and salvation through faith in Jesus Christ and that Christianity becomes a vital reality in the life of the individual only when he actually experiences the emancipating power of the Holy Spirit which brings joy, peace, and strength to the mind and soul. Such an experience involves more than the intellect and reason; it includes the whole man, his mind, emotions, will, and affections and is the wonderful and mysterious gift of the Holy Spirit to those who by the grace of God believe in the saving merits of Christ.

Both Hedberg and Rosenius were critical of the old orthodoxy which tended to make faith and reason synonymous terms and obscured the distinction between law and gospel. Both men were also impatient with the established Lutheran church in their respective lands, since it often seemed more concerned with its own institutional well-being than with the welfare of the souls of men. Both men sought to make the Bible and the historic Lutheran confessions meaningful to both clergy and laymen. Both men also agreed that the instrument by which God's rich gifts of Word, sacrament, and confession are inculcated into human hearts is the Christian church. This is the purpose and goal of the church, they said; for this the church had been established, and for this it exists. When the church occupies itself with other interests and concerns which hinder or detract from this primary goal, the church is no longer faithful to its divine purpose and must be corrected, reformed, and purified. Such reformation is not of men but of God, for the Christian church is in very truth a divine institution, divinely conceived, divinely given, and divinely guided and preserved on earth so that not even the gates of hell shall prevail against it. Within the embrace of the church the Holy Spirit calls all believers to serve God in accordance with the gifts he has bestowed.[23]

In broad outline this was essentially the theological viewpoint of Eric Norelius. His starting point was Scripture. He held that the living and eternal God speaks to man and declares the truth concerning human existence and destiny in his Word. This divine truth involves the revelation of man's sin and alienation from God, and God's astonishing response in love and the offer of salvation.

It is through faith that man lays hold of the salvation which Jesus Christ has wrought through his incarnation, his perfect obedience, his innocent sufferings and death, and his glorious resurrec-

---

[23] For a general survey of the revival movement see E. J. Ekman, *Inre missionens historia* (1st unabridged ed.; 3 vols.; Stockholm: Svenska Tryckeriaktiebolaget, 1896). See also C. O. Rosenius, *The Believer Free From the Law*, trans. A. Hult (Rock Island, Ill.: Augustana Book Concern, 1923). Nils Forsander, "Religious Thought and Movements of the Church of Sweden During the 19th Century," *Tidskrift för Teologi*, II (1900), 32 ff.

tion. It is faith that breaks down the wall of separation between God and man and makes reconciliation possible. Faith rests with confidence in the gracious goodness and mercy of God. But faith is itself a gift of grace; it is never a human achievement, nor a merely intellectual accomplishment. "I maintain," Norelius once wrote, "that it is impossible to believe, in the true sense of the word, merely with one's mind. Even if we had the most brilliant mind, the veil can blind the eyes of our soul. Without the Holy Spirit's illumination through word and sacrament there is no true faith."[24]

But where is God's truth to be discovered? Where can men hear the good news whence faith derives? Where on earth does the Holy Spirit most certainly confront men with his illuminating power and grace? To these questions Norelius replies, "In the Christian church." In a sermon preached at a convention of the Augustana Synod in Berlin, Illinois, 1867, Norelius indicates in some detail his conception of the nature and mission of the church. His text was Revelation 1:20, and his theme, "What is the Church of Christ on Earth?" The church, he says, is the holy and divine institution on earth which has not emerged out of historical circumstances but has been ordained of God. It embraces, in its true and genuine form, all those who believe in Jesus Christ as Savior and who have therefore been called by the Holy Spirit to constitute in the world a holy fellowship of believers, an *ecclesia*. In this holy fellowship, and indeed in each true believer, Jesus Christ dwells and sanctifies unto the purpose and will of God. Thus the *ecclesia* expresses in word and life the mind and spirit of God. Therefore, the church is properly likened to a candlestick which casts forth its gleaming light in the midst of darkness, revealing among men the blessed kingdom of our Lord. Through Word and sacrament the indwell-

---

[24] *Early Life of Eric Norelius, 1833-1862,* trans. Emeroy Johnson (Rock Island, Ill.: Augustana Book Concern, 1934), p. 54. A considerable collection of Norelius' sermons, which express his theological point of view, are preserved in the Norelius Collection, Archives, Lutheran Church in America, Rock Island, Ill.

ing Lord continually nourishes and sustains his faithful flock. Thus the church is always entirely dependent upon Christ and must continually seek his mercies in true worship and penitence.

But when the question is asked, "Why is the church on earth?" the answer must be twofold. First, through the church's ministration of Word and sacrament men are brought to salvation. Second, through the offices of the church men find opportunity for serving God; each believer is to show his faith in loving good works. And since there is a diversity of tasks, so there is also a diversity of gifts and talents. The pastor has his peculiar prerogatives, and each member has his particular responsibilities in keeping with his personal endowments. Such service is the Christian's response to God's grace, and such response is the essence of Christian obedience. Obedience, in these terms, includes all of life's relationships, and it is in this sense that the law has relevance for the Christian, for the Christian is guided, but not controlled, by the law. The controlling principle in Christian experience is love, and it is within the church that this love is fully nourished and through the church that it is best and most fully expressed. It is to this end that the church is structured, so as to give ample opportunity to both pastors and laymen, with various gifts and talents, to serve God and his kingdom in willing obedience. When this is done the church is indeed like a bright and shining light in the world of sin and darkness.[25]

In his own life and ministry Norelius exemplified and implemented this conception of Christian life in relation to the church. For example, he actively participated in the founding and organization of the Lutheran Minnesota Conference in 1858 and two years later, in 1860, of the Augustana Lutheran Synod. This he did because he was convinced that just as no individual Christian can stand alone in isolation, so neither can congregations exist apart

[25] *Protokoll*, Augustana Synod, 1867. Norelius' debate with Gustaf Unonius, the Swedish Episcopal missionary, recorded in *Tidskrift för Teologi*, I (1899), pp. 15 ff., sheds further light on his view of the church.

from other like-minded congregations. It is the genius of Christianity that it draws believers together in common bonds of faith and devotion and in the accomplishment of acts of serving love.[26] Norelius' stature as a churchman is nowhere more evident than in the service which he rendered in the development of a suitable and workable church polity. In the second volume of his monumental *Historia* he recalls how the early Scandinavian congregations struggled to devise a type of structure and government which would best serve the needs of people in an American environment.[27] Association with other midwestern Lutherans in the Synod of Northern Illinois from 1851 to 1860 afforded the Scandinavian congregations almost a decade of valuable experience in the organization and management of a free church in a pluralistic society. But it was men like Norelius who played the chief role as architects, giving shape and form to the emerging institutions which the Scandinavian settlers were providing for themselves in the New World.

In the first half-century of the life of the Augustana Synod, Eric Norelius was a member of practically every important commission and committee which formulated the polity and policies of the synod, its conferences, and its institutions. He was a member of the constitution committee of the Minnesota Conference in 1858 and of the revision committee of 1871. He was chairman of the committee which formulated the constitution for St. Ansgar's Academy in 1863 and headed the committee on constitution for the succeeding institution, Gustavus Adolphus College, in 1874. He was a member of the committee that drew up the original rules governing the Augustana Pension and Aid Fund in 1867. He served on the committee which created the first form for pastoral calls to be issued by congregations. He was chairman of the committee of the Augustana Synod which worked out new procedures for the reor-

---

[26] For Norelius' discussion of this point see his *De Svenska Luterska Församlingarnas och Svenskarnes Historia i Amerika,* I, 773 f. On the organization of the Minnesota Conference see *Tidskrift för Teologi,* I (1899), 133 ff.
[27] Vol. II, pp. 237 ff.

ganization and management of home missions in 1870. In the same
year the synod adopted a revised congregational constitution which
had been proposed by Norelius. This constitution was revised in
1894, and again Norelius had an important part in framing the
new formula.

At the constituting convention of the Augustana Synod in 1860
it was Norelius who proposed the creation of a Home Mission
Board, the purpose of which was to initiate and supervise a synodical home missions program aimed particularly at the increasing
number of Scandinavian immigrants coming to America. To that
end the Board was authorized to call a traveling missionary whose
responsibility it would be to seek out new Scandinavian settlements
in the Mississippi Valley and elsewhere, and wherever possible to
organize congregations and relate them to the Augustana Synod.[28]

The first candidate called to the post of traveling missionary
declined the offer, whereupon the synod turned to Eric Norelius,
who was at the time serving the Swedish congregation in Attica,
Indiana. He accepted the call and prepared immediately to move
to the Minnesota Territory. He thus became the first traveling
missionary of the Augustana Synod. Serving the little Swedish
congregation in St. Paul as time would allow, he spent the next
year journeying in all kinds of weather to various parts of the
Minnesota country in search of scattered countrymen, preaching,
teaching, baptizing, confirming, burying, marrying, and organizing
congregations where possible. His vivid description of the hazards
and hardships he encountered as he drove his old blind horse
through dense forests, deep snow, and uncharted wilderness is a
saga of great drama and interest.

Having served a year as traveling missionary Norelius resigned
and accepted a call to the Vasa-Red Wing parish in Minnesota,
where he remained for the next six years. Indeed, though he served
the Augustana Synod in various capacities which at times took him

---

[28] See *Protokoll,* Augustana Synod, 1860, p. 11.

far from Vasa in the ensuing years, he established his permanent home in the little town of Vasa and served as the pastor of the Vasa congregation for five different terms.

Whether traveling missionary or resident pastor, his ministry was always characterized by a high regard for churchly order and an emphasis upon Christian nurture. In order to reach his people more directly he made use of various techniques which had been developed in the evangelical revivals in Sweden. The informal Bible study and prayer session, called a conventicle, was a regular part of Norelius' program. He also conducted catechetical sessions in the homes of his parishioners during which the doctrines of the church would be reviewed, discussed, and explained. The emphasis at these *husförhör*, as they were called, was not upon an intellectualized Christianity but upon a biblically oriented knowledge of the doctrines of sin and grace, leading to a personal experience of the forgiveness of sins and commitment of life to God. It was particularly at this point that Norelius reveals his indebtedness to Hedberg and Rosenius.

Endeavoring to supplement and reinforce his own teaching ministry, Norelius established both Sunday and parochial schools in his congregations and urged other pastors to do likewise. The recruitment of spiritually mature men and women to conduct these schools was an important concern in the ministry of Norelius. Here was a challenging opportunity for lay people to serve God's kingdom within the structured life of the church; and to do so was, according to Norelius, both a Christian's duty and privilege. It was in this same conviction that he also established a women's missionary society in his Vasa congregation, the purpose of which was to give women an opportunity to invest their personal time and talents in support of Christian causes, especially Christian education. Norelius held that Christians are called not only to receive, but also to give; to provide opportunity and guidance for such giving was a prime responsibility of the church and its clergy.

Norelius was careful to nurture his congregations in the traditions of the Lutheran church. To this end he carefully followed the prescribed order and practice of the Augustana Synod. He once stated his own position in these words:

> . . . my own way of procedure may be considered too churchly by some, since I very carefully follow the ritual [liturgy] of our church, and I cannot deny that in outward appearance, garb, etc., I like to be somewhat ministerial, as far as I can understand it. I also become more and more convinced that form, though it is not and never can be essential, still is of no little importance for religion.[20]

In general it might be said that the churchmanship of Eric Norelius tended neither to the right nor to the left, neither to low nor to high church practice, but kept rather to a conservative middle ground. This was perhaps due not only to his theological and ecclesiastical convictions, but also to his own natural inclinations, for Norelius was not a bold or imaginative man; he seems rather to have been a somewhat stolid individual who preferred the peace and tranquility of tradition to the risks and excitement of experimentation. In his relations with his contemporaries he enjoyed the respect and esteem of many, and the suspicion and mistrust of a few. In the early years of his ministry he sustained a somewhat ambiguous relationship to the synod because of his opposition to a strong centralized synodical authority. As the pioneer and leader of the church in Minnesota, he encouraged a spirit of independence on the part of the regional conferences with a consequent weakening of synodical authority. His efforts to establish an independent Minnesota Conference school, an independent Minnesota press, and an independent eleemosynary work were interpreted by friends and foes alike as a move in the direction of

[20] Emeroy Johnson, *Eric Norelius* (Rock Island, Ill.: Augustana Book Concern, 1954), p. 141.

founding an independent, autonomous Minnesota Synod. But when he was elected to his first term as president of the Augustana Synod in 1874, serving for seven consecutive years in that office until 1881, he threw his influence on the side of a strong synod, urging that regional loyalties be subordinated to the greater, more comprehensive synodical support. He thus left to his erstwhile Minnesota colleagues, such as Peter Sjöblom, Andrew Jackson, Peter Carlson, and P. A. Cedarstam, the unenviable burden of continuing the battle for conference versus synodical sovereignty, opposed now by the very man who had once been their leader in this venture.

By the time the Augustana Synod called Norelius to the synodical helm for the second time in 1899, continuing to elect him year after year until 1911, the strife between conference and synod had been resolved by the adoption of a new synodical constitution in 1894. This new constitution delegated chief responsibility for the exercise of authority and direction to the synod, but provided equal conference representation in all synodical decisions and actions.

Humanitarian and Educator

Frederick Jackson Turner has pointed out that the frontier in America constituted the meeting place between savagery and civilization.[30] In the transformation of the American environment from savagery to civilization no factor was more important than religion. Into the raw and often lawless circumstances of the frontier, the pioneer pastors came preaching respect for law and order, concern for the welfare of neighbors, and appreciation for knowledge and learning. Though it must be admitted that the cause of religion was sometimes represented by men who substituted emo-

[30] Frederick Jackson Turner, *Frontier and Section: Selected Essays* (Englewood Cliffs, N. J.: Prentice-Hall, 1961), p. 38.

tional extravagance for theological training, it must nevertheι be said that it was the church which not only championed decency and order, but also became the earliest mother of public welfare and education.

In this respect the ministry of Eric Norelius was characteristic of the pioneer clergyman. He was an advocate of law and order and the founder of important eleemosynary and educational institutions.

As the advocate of law, order, and public decency Norelius faced a real challenge among his scattered countrymen in Minnesota. There was more than enough rowdyism, vulgarity, and chicanery in the Scandinavian settlements he served. In his *Journals* he frequently complains about the discouraging worldliness and spiritual indifference of the people, even among members of his own flock. In one congregation, he claimed that there were certain men, "officers of the congregation, who have even wanted to have the pastor along at their card games and drinking parties."[31] Norelius did not take this as a compliment to his own popularity but saw it as an evidence of low moral deportment and a deplorable estimate of the pastor's place in the community. He also records the fact that it was a member of his congregation in St. Paul who swindled him out of thirty-five dollars in gold by selling him a stolen horse and wagon, which were subsequently seized by the sheriff, leaving Norelius stranded on one of his early missionary journeys into the Minnesota interior.[32]

A man with Norelius' stern sense of Christian duty and moral accountability and his pietistic aversion to "worldliness" had some emphatic things to say to such erring sheep about the "wages of sin" and the certainty of divine retribution. That he did not spare the rod when he felt such measures were called for is evident both

[31] *Journals,* p. 153 below.
[32] Johnson, *Early Life,* pp. 287 f.

in the sermons he preached and the reports which he submitted as president of the Minnesota Conference and the Augustana Synod.[33]

It was Norelius' endeavors as a humanitarian and educator, however, that gave a special luster and significance to his ministry. His humanitarian leadership first came into prominence in 1862 in connection with the Indian uprising in Minnesota that year. For a number of years the Sioux tribes, concentrated in the Yellow Medicine Reservation in the west-central section of the territory, had been nursing a growing resentment against the white settlers. By devious means the Indians had been tricked into agreements which deprived them of their ancestral hunting grounds without receiving fair and equitable recompense. Step by step the white man had crowded the Indian out of his homelands, pushing him into an ever smaller territory, hedging him about with laws and rules the Indian did not want and could not understand. Growing more and more resentful as they watched the increasing encroachments, the Sioux finally decided to drive their white enemies from the territory west of the Mississippi.

The Sioux hit the warpath on August 17, 1862, striking settlements first in Meeker County, Minnesota, and then spreading their assault quickly in all directions; they reached as far north as Kandiyohi County and southward into the upper reaches of Nicollet County. Hundreds of people were killed, and some women and children were taken captive. Churches, houses, and barns were burned, crops destroyed, and cattle and horses dispersed or stolen. A number of border settlements were completely wiped out, while others were partially destroyed. Virtually the entire population in the stricken area was forced to flee on foot across the country, seeking shelter and help wherever they could be found. Among the

[33] See President's reports, *Protokoll, Minnesota Konferensen,* 1872, 1873, 1874, 1895; *Protokoll,* Augustana Synod, 1875-1881; 1900-1911. Sermons in full manuscript and outline form, testifying to Norelius' stern warnings to his people, are preserved in the Norelius Collection, LCA Archives, Rock Island, Ill.

hapless victims were many who were members of devastated Swedish Lutheran congregations at Nest Lake, Norway Lake, Eagle Lake, and elsewhere.

When the news of this tragedy reached other sections of the country, even though no appeal for relief funds had been made, voluntary offerings from friends in Minnesota, Illinois, Indiana, and Iowa began to pour into the hands of Eric Norelius, who was the most widely-known pastor in the area. The Minnesota Conference elected a special relief committee, headed by Norelius, to supervise the aid program to victims of the massacre. Within a few months almost seven hundred and fifty dollars had been received, and aid had been extended to approximately seventy families. At the same time devastated congregations were reorganized and re-established, and church structures which had been damaged or destroyed were rebuilt. In this entire undertaking it was Eric Norelius who took command of the situation. He handled the relief funds, supervised and coordinated various phases of the program, and acted as the chief agent for both the conference and the synod in channeling aid and assistance to the needy.[34]

Norelius undertook an even more important humanitarian project in 1865, when he established the first Lutheran children's home in Minnesota. Inspiration for such a project seems to have come to him first through the influence of William A. Passavant, of Pittsburgh, founder of a number of Lutheran eleemosynary institutions and of the Lutheran diaconate in America. The decision of the Augustana Synod to establish a children's home in Illinois may also have influenced Norelius.[35] The circumstances which

[34] Vivid accounts of the Indian uprising and the steps taken to alleviate the suffering appeared in *Hemlandet*, the Swedish journal, August 27, September 3, and November 5, 1862. See also *Protokoll, Minnesota Konferensen*, October 8, 1862, printed in *Tidskrift för Teologi*, I (1899), 171. Norelius, *Historia*, II, 145.

[35] The Rev. William A. Passavant visited Minnesota in the summer of 1856. During this visit he was a guest in the log cabin home of young Norelius, who now had opportunity to hear at first hand of the great humanitarian ac-

afforded Norelius the occasion for implementing his dream of a children's home in Minnesota was the untimely death of Eric Erson and his wife Anna, who had recently come from Sweden. While making their home temporarily in St. Paul, both parents took sick and died, leaving four surviving children without home or money. There were two boys, aged twelve and six, and two girls, aged ten and five. The two youngest were placed in the Protestant Orphan Asylum in St. Paul, while Eric Norelius brought the two oldest ones to his home in Red Wing and appealed to his congregation for help in caring for them. A room in the undercroft of the Vasa church was furnished and equipped as a home, and a widow, Brita Nilson, was engaged as housemother and cook. Thus originated the Vasa Children's Home, which was destined in the years to come to serve scores of homeless children. For the first eleven years of its existence this institution remained the personal project and responsibility of Eric Norelius. It was not until 1876 that the Minnesota Conference was persuaded to assume responsibility for the home. In giving his first report regarding his venture in social missions to the synod at large through the columns of *Hemlandet,* Norelius declared:

> Without any particular difficulty we have so far received what we have needed to give them food and clothing. Many of the members of the congregation have provided the little household with flour, potatoes, meat, butter, eggs, milk, etc., and other minor items as they have been able, and this without my saying anything about it. . . . The household may become larger this fall, but we hope the income will also increase. Our plans for the future are very simple. We intend, if possible, to get a house which the institution can call its own, and then we intend to accept all the destitute who really need a home. The matter is really in the hands of God.[36]

tivities of Passavant. The resolution to establish an orphans' home in Illinois was adopted by the Augustana Synod at its annual convention in 1863; see *Protokoll,* Augustana Synod, 1863, p. 8. For an appraisal of the rivalry between Norelius and his Illinois colleagues, see G. Everett Arden, *Augustana Heritage,* pp. 81 ff.; 102 f.; 115 ff.

[36] *Hemlandet,* October 2, 1866.

By 1867 the "household" had increased so that Norelius found it necessary to purchase ten acres of land near the Vasa church and to erect a dormitory to house the growing family of homeless children. Now with a home of its own the Vasa orphanage was able to extend its services to a larger number of unfortunate boys and girls. Maintaining a wholesome Christian environment for scores of children who otherwise might have suffered serious deprivation, the Vasa Home became a model for other children's homes which were subsequently established throughout the Augustana Synod in the years that followed.

Although the humanitarian endeavors of Norelius constituted a significant phase of his ministry, his unique contribution was undoubtedly in the field of education. And in this case education must be conceived in broad terms to include not only institutions of formal education, but also the educational influence exerted through the written word.

Even by the standards of that early pioneer period, Eric Norelius was not a highly educated man. It must be admitted that his course of study in preparation for the ministry had been somewhat haphazard. He might well have been expected to succumb to the pressures of a frontier environment which so frequently demanded religious enthusiasm rather than knowledge and understanding. But Eric Norelius was the heir of a tradition which emphasized the necessity for an educated clergy and an informed laity. Esteem for learning was in his blood, and therefore as a poverty-stricken immigrant youth he grasped the opportunities which were afforded him to absorb as excellent an education as possible. Even with his meager academic background he disciplined himself at Capital University in the study not only of the practical courses but in the more rigorous areas of biblical language and exegesis.

He shared with his older colleague, L. P. Esbjörn, the conviction that the future of the Lutheran church in North America depended upon the nurture and training of an indigenous American Lutheran clergy and the fostering of a knowledgeable Lutheran constituency. The disastrous experience of the Swedish Lutherans on the Delaware in the previous century, when there had been too much dependence upon resources drawn from Europe, haunted the minds of men like Esbjörn and Norelius. While a colonial church might possibly survive for a time without providing for its perpetuation, as the Delaware Swedes indeed had, an immigrant church without European backing would be doomed to almost immediate extinction unless it could furnish for itself the means for its own growth and development. When Esbjörn dreamed and planned for the day when the Scandinavians would have their own schools in America, he had no more eager listener or ardent supporter than Eric Norelius. Indeed, while still a student at Capital University, Norelius expressed the hope that the Scandinavians would soon be able to provide an education for their own people which would more adequately and faithfully express the Scandinavian ethos than that which prevailed in Columbus.[37]

The opportunity to implement his convictions was not presented to Norelius until he had settled in Minnesota and assumed leadership of the work in that area. As the stream of Scandinavian immigration turned increasingly in the direction of the upper midwest, more and more Lutheran congregations were organized throughout the southern and central sections of the Minnesota Territory. As the population grew and the number of congregations increased, the sectional needs of this part of Scandinavian Lutheranism became more apparent and more acute. While the older Swedish settlements in Illinois claimed the prerogatives of leadership and expected the newer settlements in Minnesota and elsewhere to look to them for guidance, the difficulties imposed by long distances and primitive transportation and communications facilities served to encourage the growth of sectional independence and self-reliance.

[37] Cf. Norelius, *Historia*, II, 258.

Although the Scandinavians in the midwest had united in support of the small college and seminary established at Springfield, Illinois, in 1852, talk of an independent educational institution which would better serve the regional interests of the upper midwest was being heard in Minnesota as early as 1856. In that year Norelius was approached by two laymen, Peter Carlson and Halvor Strand, with the suggestion that Norelius should sponsor the establishment of a training school, perhaps in his own home, where interested young men from Minnesota might pursue studies in preparation for service in the church as teachers and pastors. In the summer of that same year Passavant made his visit to Minnesota. During his sojourn he conferred with Norelius and broached the subject of an independent Minnesota Synod as well as a school for the territory. For the time being, however, nothing came of these proposals.

The time for action came when the Minnesota Conference met for its annual convention in 1862, at East Union. After serious discussion of the educational needs of the area, the following resolution was adopted:

> That, since the need for teachers in our congregations is so pressing that we can no longer bear it, it is hereby decided that Brother Norelius be requested to assume the task of instructing such young men as the congregations might send to him. Brother Norelius accepted this assignment.[38]

As a consequence of this conference action Norelius opened his home in Red Wing, Minnesota, in the fall of 1862 to a number of young men who now began their studies under Norelius' tutelage. In this quiet manner the first Lutheran school in Minnesota was launched under the name of Minnesota Elementar Läroverk ("Minnesota Elementary School"). That there was a real need for

[38] Copy of Minnesota Conference Minutes in *Tidskrift för Teologi,* I (1899), 171.

such a school is evident from the fact that within a few months the student body numbered about a dozen young men. Since the Minnesota Conference had appropriated no money, elected no supervisory board, nor made any arrangements for future action regarding this educational venture, the school was in fact the personal responsibility of Eric Norelius to carry out as he saw fit. During the first year he not only supplied classroom space in his own home, but arranged the curriculum, ordered the necessary textbooks, and conducted all classes himself.

When the school was later moved to Carver, Minnesota, and installed in a small log house near the Carver church, Norelius engaged the Rev. Andrew Jackson to assume leadership of the institution, which was now known as St. Ansgar's Academy. In 1875 the school was moved to its permanent home in St. Peter, and its name changed to Gustavus Adolphus College. During these years, however, no one in Minnesota played a more active or important role in the direction of the school than Eric Norelius. After relinquishing his teaching duties when the school was moved to Carver, Norelius continued to serve as a member of the school board for many years and actively engaged in efforts to acquire both adequate funds and competent teachers for the institution.

Closely connected with Norelius' concern for education was his literary interest. Just as he saw the need for educated pastors and teachers, so he also perceived the need for an informed laity. He sought to meet the latter need by his literary endeavors.

His first literary venture was launched in the fall of 1857 when he began publication of a Swedish newspaper *Minnesota Posten*. The first issue announced the aims of the paper to be the dissemination of information, particularly to the people of Minnesota, regarding both public and churchly matters. While the editorial policy would be independent of party affiliation, the editor found himself at the moment favoring the political principles of the Republican party. He would therefore support the program of that party, at least for the present. The readers were told that they could expect articles dealing with news in the areas of science, art, economics, and world events. As for religion, the paper and its editor would be unreservedly on the side of orthodox, conservative Lutheranism.

Norelius continued to publish his newspaper until October, 1858, when the financial burdens of this venture could no longer be borne, and although he had some three hundred subscribers he found it necessary to suspend publication. The synodical newspaper, *Hemlandet,* which the Rev. T. N. Hasselquist had been publishing in Galesburg, Illinois, since 1855, now moved its editorial offices to Chicago and called Norelius as editor. This call was accepted, and Norelius now became the editor of the journal which he had so recently regarded as his arch rival in the literary field. Due to disagreement with the former editor of *Hemlandet,* however, Norelius resigned within a few months and assumed charge of a congregation in Attica, Indiana.

For the next ten years, 1860 to 1870, Norelius did not again venture into the newspaper field. But in January, 1870, he again found himself at the editor's desk of a periodical, this one devoted to the cause of home and foreign missions. Although he continued in this position for only two years, it marked the beginning of a twelve-year period when Norelius' pen was constantly busy, for during this time he was associated with the editorship of no fewer than four different periodicals.[39]

It was as the historian of the Augustana Synod, however, that Norelius rendered his greatest literary service to the church. From the time he landed in America as a young immigrant, he seems to have been conscious of the fact that he was participating in events of historic importance. His personal diary, kept from early youth

---

[39] Norelius was editor of the following papers: *Missionaren,* 1870-1871; *Luthersk Kyrkotidning,* 1872-1873; *Evangelisk Luthersk Tidskrift,* 1877; *Skaffaren,* 1878-1882.

to old age, his voluminous file of carefully preserved personal correspondence, his notes on early Scandinavian settlements in America, his meticulous records of missionary journeys, of the establishing of congregations, and of ecclesiastical meetings and decisions, together with his collection of biographical accounts of outstanding clerical leaders of the church all attest to Norelius' unusual historical interest.

It was because of his well-known interest in history that the Augustana Synod in 1866 elected Norelius to head a special committee to gather and preserve historical documents relating to the origins of the synod in America. Three years later the synod designated Norelius as the official historian of the church, and asked him to prepare an account of the synod's various activities for use in missionary work among the Swedish immigrants.[40] When Norelius accepted this assignment, it marked the beginning of a literary career as church historian which covered almost a half-century. For the rest of his life, as time and strength would allow, Norelius was almost constantly at work on some phase of historical research or writing pertaining either to the Augustana Synod or to the Minnesota Conference. His *magnum opus* is the monumental two-volume history of Swedish Lutheranism in America covering 1,412 pages and entitled *De Svenska Luterska Församlingarnas och Svenskarnes Historia i Amerika,*[41] which begins with an account of the earliest Swedish settlements in America during the nineteenth century and concludes with the period just prior to World War I. These volumes constitute the most complete study ever written of the Swedish Lutheran tradition in America. And although the work suffers at a number of points from Norelius' lack of formal training in historiography, it is nevertheless an invaluable record of an important phase of American Lutheranism.

[40] *Protokoll,* Augustana Synod, 1866, 1869.
[41] Rock Island, Ill.: Lutheran Augustana Book Concern, 1890, 1916. The work has never been translated. The excerpts that appear in the present volume have been translated by the editor.

In the later years of his life Norelius was persuaded to write an account of his experiences as a pioneer pastor on the American frontier. These somewhat rambling memoirs were published in serial form in the Swedish journal *Augustana* in 1930 and 1931 under the title "Några Minnesteckningar: Självbiografi av Erik Norelius." Translated into English by the Rev. Emeroy Johnson, these articles appeared as a serial in the *Lutheran Companion* in 1933 and 1934, and then in book form under the title *Early Life of Eric Norelius, 1833-1862* (Rock Island, Ill.: Augustana Book Concern, 1934).

In connection with his historical writing, Norelius sought to awaken through historical knowledge a deeper appreciation of, and a more vital commitment throughout the Augustana Synod to, the religious and spiritual heritage embodied in and expressed through this church. To that end he was untiring in his efforts to urge pastors, congregations, and conferences to gather and preserve important historical materials for future reference. In this way he did much to inspire the establishment of archival depositories on the part of the synod and several of the conferences. Through his historical activities he bequeathed to future generations a perspective which provided both understanding and appreciation for a religious heritage which is rich and enduring.

The death of Eric Norelius on March 15, 1916, marked the end of an era. He was the last of the pioneer pastors who had participated in the founding of the Augustana Lutheran Synod at Jefferson Prairie, Wisconsin, in June, 1860. He was one of the last of the intrepid frontier missionaries who had matched the hardships and deprivations of pioneer life with their courage and determination, their faith and devotion to Christ and his church. His life spanned the time between the frontier days and the modern era of the church in America.

Perhaps no more fitting epitaph could be given to this long life of Christian service than was written by Norelius himself in the concluding paragraphs of his *Historia*: "The times change, and we change with them . . . but truth, as given to us in God's own Word and in our Lutheran confessions, does not change; of this heritage we can yield nothing, come what may."[42]

*   *   *

No complete series of Norelius' journals seems to be extant. The personal records of Norelius are to be found in the archives of both Gustavus Adolphus College, St. Peter, Minnesota, and the Lutheran Church in America, Rock Island, Illinois. The journals here presented are preserved in the latter depository.

The text that follows constitutes a somewhat abridged translation of the Swedish original, with references to the weather, daily chores, and other matters of little or no general interest omitted. The annotation, the chapter headings, and the subheadings have been supplied by the editor.

[42] *Historia*, II, 527.

THE JOURNALS
OF
ERIC NORELIUS

1

EARLY YEARS AND EMIGRATION[1]

1833-1851

I, Eric Norelius, was born about midnight, October 26, 1833, on the Eric Anders farm in Norrbäck, Hassela parish, in northern Halsingland, Sweden, during the reign of King Charles XIV.[2] My father, Andrew Persson, a farmer, and my mother, Lina Jönsdotter, were both born in Hassela parish of poor but pious peasant stock.[3] My maternal grandmother was of Finnish extraction. At the time of their marriage my parents had very little in earthly goods. They lived first in Berenget, but later moved to the Eric Anders farm in Norrbäck. They toiled diligently on the farm and managed to achieve a measure of security, although they were heavily burdened with debts.

My parents are true Christians. They believe that they are for-

[1] Norelius began his *Minnesbok* or daily journal in the summer of 1850 as a way of occupying a part of the tedious journey across the Atlantic to America. As an introduction to this *Minnesbok,* he wrote a brief personal history of his childhood in Sweden. The journal proper begins after the subheading "From Sweden to Andover."

[2] Halsingland is located in the eastern section of north-central Sweden. King Charles XIV John was the royal name taken by the brilliant French marshal, Jean Baptiste Bernadotte (1763-1844), when he accepted the Swedish invitation to become heir to the Swedish crown in 1810. His coronation took place on May 11, 1818.

[3] For purposes of easier identification many Scandinavian immigrants adopted a new family name upon coming to America. Thus Eric dropped the family name of Persson and took the name of Norelius. Other members of his family followed his example upon their arrival in America.

given and saved for the sake of Jesus Christ, through grace and not by their own works. I have seven brothers and sisters, three older and four younger than I. The oldest is Peter, now married to Anna Schmidt; next is Jonas, married to Lina Olofsdotter; then there is Andrew, who is now in America. The younger ones include Caren, Olof, Juliana, and Lars. My brothers and sisters thought of me as something of a cut-up and the most mulish and stubborn of the lot, and they were doubtless right.

The village of Norrbäck is very lovely. A hilly ridge running along the northern edge of the neighborhood is covered with thick woods, and here in these hills I spent many happy hours of my childhood. Up there in the hills, especially in the springtime when the barren trees were being clothed again in new, green foliage, my heart would be strangely lifted, and the dark, cold winter was easily forgotten. From my earliest years and until about the age of twelve, most of my time was spent playing with the other children. Even in these early years, however, I occasionally entertained thoughts about eternity and other religious matters. I clearly remember when my mother once spoke to me about the blessings of heaven. I could not have been more than four years old, but I still recall that I was sitting near the fireplace in the old house and that my dear mother sat beside me as she sewed and conversed with her little son. Her sweet words concerning the joys of heaven made a deep impression upon me, and even then I resolved so to live that I, too, would some day share the joys of heaven. And I must confess that though I have often fallen into grievous sin and error, my conscience which was awakened in those early days has never been dormant.

When I was about five years old I began to show an interest in reading and writing and soon acquired some knowledge of these arts. By the time I was six or seven I had exhibited some flair for study. In spite of my older brother's objections, I made surreptitious use of his pencils, papers, and school books. By the time I was eight years old I was able to read Luther's Small Catechism with explanations by A. J. Lindblom.[4] As a reward for this achievement I received a small tin watch from my father.

By the time I had reached nine years of age I was sent out, together with my older brother Andrew, to herd sheep and goats. A year later I was given this task to do alone, and continued with this work every summer until 1848. During the winters my brothers and I were expected to help Father operate the charcoal kiln. I did not enjoy this kind of work and my father was almost obliged to force me to do it. My thought seemed constantly to be centered on my studies and on plans to further my education. In these plans I met the firm opposition of my father, who sought by all means to encourage me to become a laborer instead of a scholar, but his efforts were in vain.

Finally, in the spring of 1847, after gaining the reluctant consent of my parents, I enrolled as a young pupil in the local parish school. Here was an environment in which I thrived, and although it may sound like boasting, I must confess that I made rapid progress in my studies. Mr. Olof Schönberg, the local schoolmaster, observing my diligence and natural abilities, encouraged me, and said that I must go on with my studies and enroll in the high school at Hudiksvall.[5] To this I readily agreed and asked him to try to persuade my parents to give their consent. This he succeeded in doing although it turned out to be a most difficult undertaking. I vividly recall the day my father promised me that I could enroll at Hudiksvall. We were cutting wood out in the forest and were conversing about my education. He explained to me that his reluctance regarding my schooling was due only to a

---

[4] This should read J. A. Lindblom, archbishop of Sweden and author of a catechism published in 1810.

[5] Hudiksvall is a port city on the east coast of north-central Sweden.

lack of money. Nevertheless, I was to be permitted the opportunity of trying my hand at higher studies in the Hudiksvall school, and Father expressed the hope that the Lord would provide the necessary means for my continued education. It was agreed that I would not be able to enroll for the fall term, but the necessary arrangements would certainly be made for enrollment at the spring term. It was with the greatest joy that I received this parental promise, and I immediately began to entertain the highest hopes for my future. From my earliest childhood I had thought about the holy ministry, but now I began to give this subject more serious consideration than ever before in the expectation that I would in due time attain this high goal. Now I was at peace with myself and eagerly awaited the day when I could enter high school. In the meantime my dear parents made all necessary arrangements for my stay at Hudiksvall, a city which lies some seven Swedish miles from my parental home.

Education in Sweden

The long awaited day finally dawned when my dear father hitched up the horses, drove me to Hudiksvall, and enrolled me as a student in the high school.[6] It was February 6, 1849. During the first term I boarded in the home of my uncle, while I occupied a room in the home of Jonas Hedlund, a family with whom I spent many happy hours.

My first teacher was Axel Jennische, an exceptionally fine man with a kind and patient disposition. My next instructor was Jacob Hallgren from Ljusdalen, a strict disciplinarian who nevertheless favored those who diligently studied their lessons. In the beginning I was enrolled in the so-called primary class. The first term ended June 14, 1849, and the cost to my parents amounted to

[6] This was the "gymnasium," the next step in Swedish education following completion of the elementary grades.

eighty-five rix-dollars.[7] At the close of the school year my father brought me back home.

During the summer of 1849 I was lazy and did very little work, neglecting even my books and studies. But I was experiencing at that time a very severe inner spiritual struggle. It seemed to me that during recent years the Lutheran teachings had been weakened and watered down in Sweden as well as in Norway, Denmark, and Finland. The outstanding scholars of the day seemed to be giving the Bible a rationalistic interpretation and espoused a system of doctrine which included the following emphases: the individual who falls into sin thereby breaks his baptismal covenant and renders his baptism invalid. He must now make a completely new beginning, effecting his salvation by his own works and deeds. He must be awakened, whereupon he must struggle against sin and evil, always obeying the right and the good. But this is precisely what he is unable to do by himself. He must therefore watch, pray, and persevere until God in mercy comes to him and bestows the gift of faith and salvation.[8]

Now, all this sounds reasonable and natural and is easily understood. But when God's Word speaks of the sinner it plainly states that unless he believes in the forgiveness of sins through Jesus Christ he is lost. A young pastor in Finland who has become the leader and chief spokesman for a type of piety which was exceptionally critical of the established churches in Scandinavia and of their clergy has opposed the popular rationalism of the day and has published a newspaper and several books to inform the common people regarding this threat to the gospel.[9] His writings

---

[7] The rix-dollar was a standard Swedish coin until about 1855, when it was displaced by the *krona* or crown. The rix-dollar was worth about four crowns. The current value of the Swedish crown is approximately twenty cents in American money.

[8] In a marginal note which Norelius apparently made in his *Journals* years later he says, "When this was written I was a rather strict Norrland pietist."

[9] The man to whom reference is made was Frederick Gabriel Hedberg (1811-1893).

have been very widely received and have created both supporters and opponents. Throughout Helsingland and in other Swedish provinces he has many followers as well as enemies. My own family and relatives have eagerly received his teachings, which are none other than the pure doctrines of Luther.

During the summer, while I was at home, I read with deepest interest the books of this man and was very impressed with his viewpoint. I came to the firm conviction that for Christ's sake I am saved just as I am if I truly believe in Christ as Savior. Now I had a peaceful conscience in the knowledge that I had found in Christ a gracious God. It occurred to me that the surroundings at school were not in accordance with God's spirit and will, and the more I thought about the matter the more I found myself dreading the prospect of returning for the fall term. I pondered the possibility of finding a private tutor, but this proved impossible. In the fall, therefore, my faithful father drove me and my cousin Jonas Engberg back to school, which began on September 6, 1849. Both Engberg and I were enrolled in the second class. I studied with such exceptional diligence that at the end of the term I was promoted to the third class.

During the Christmas recess I requested help from my home parish for support during the next school term. This request was granted. I was the only student from the Hassela parish and planned to continue my education even though I was unhappy about the conditions at school. In preparation for Christmas I learned to chant the Christmas Epistle to the best of my ability, and on Christmas Day I participated in the service by chanting the Epistle for the day in the Hassela parish church. I suspect that it was not a particularly polished performance. After Christmas my father, sometimes accompanied by my brother Jonas, took me around in the parish, where I sang from house to house, asking the people to give me some small gift of grain, bread, sausage, meat, wool, linen, etc., for my support while at school. When I was finished the total value of my collection amounted to only forty-two rix-dollars.

While at home during the Christmas recess I diligently read the Scriptures, and this awakened in me once more a deep loathing for school. It was with the greatest difficulty, however, that I admitted to my parents that I now wanted to quit school since I had earlier been so adamant about enrolling. They understood my feelings about the conditions at school and my lack of sufficient funds, but voiced the hope that circumstances would improve and that ways and means could be found to enable me to continue. They suggested that I must decide either to go to work as a laborer or return to school. These were the alternatives. Reluctantly I decided to return to school.

Both of my parents accompanied me to the city since they were to do some shopping in preparation for the weddings of my two older brothers, who planned to be married during the coming Easter season. Having again arrived in Hudiksvall, there welled up within me such an aversion for school that I determined not to return to classes, come what may. The very morning that classes were to resume I arose very early before my parents had left the city, and going to them I demanded permission to quit school. This parental confrontation was not so difficult as I had feared. I assured them that I intended to continue my studies under private tutorship, which would require even greater diligence and application on my part than would be needed in class attendance. My parents, who were unacquainted with school matters, had very little to say, so they returned home, leaving me in Hudiksvall. After their departure I sought out some friends, from whom I borrowed a few books, but I did not bother about finding a private tutor. Pursuing my studies privately I continued in this situation until a couple of weeks before Easter, when my two older brothers arrived in the city to shop for their approaching weddings. When they returned home, I accompanied them but was given a rather cool reception by my parents.

At home again I busied myself with studies in Latin, German, the Bible, and other subjects. Meanwhile I was thinking about going to America, but shared such thoughts with no one. The question of the cost of such a journey posed a real problem since I had no resources of my own. Before their marriages my older brothers had talked about going to America, but now they had lost their wanderlust. Brother Andrew, however, remained resolute in his decision to go to America. I was now the cause of sorrow to my parents because I wanted neither to work nor to attend school. Though they would gladly have compelled me to go to school, their limited means would not permit them to support me in the city. I must confess that I was a disappointment to myself. I wanted to complete my studies and felt that this was surely God's will for me but had no idea how it could become possible. In the midst of this distress, I decided to write to the Rev. Anders Wiberg, of Söderhamm, and seek his advice, for I knew him to be perhaps the only really upright pastor in all Helsingland.[10]

Having given him a detailed account of my present circumstances, in due time I received word from him advising me to go to North America since it would doubtless be easier for a penniless student to receive an education in America than in Sweden. His letter reached me on the third Sunday after Easter, 1850. When my family read the letter they agreed that it would perhaps be best for me to follow his counsel. The entire cost of the journey to America was assumed by my indefatigable and faithful father. The fare to America for me and my brother Andrew amounted to three hundred rix-dollars. The day for our scheduled departure was awaited with eager impatience. When that day actu-

---

[10] Norelius' critical attitude toward the Swedish church and its clergy at this time and his strong puritanical tendencies reflect the prevailing spirit of much of Swedish revival piety of that day which was particularly strong in northern Sweden. The influence of Hedberg is especially evident.

ally dawned, however, it was not so delightful as had been antici-
pated but was full of sorrow and heartache.

From Sweden to Andover

It was on July 18, 1850, that we left our parental home, and
I shall remember that day as long as I live. I had not the slightest
inclination to leave. I wept bitterly, and indeed my whole family
was in tears, both old and young. It was more like death than
life in my home that day, because we were now to part from one
another, perhaps never to meet again in this life on earth. This
at least seemed to be the likeliest prospect. Oh, what anguish I
suffered as I embraced my brothers and sisters for what might well
be the last time and bade them farewell! And then my poor, dear
mother followed us to the churchyard so that she could truthfully
say that in this last moment she had brought us alive to the very
portals of the church. Oh, what a painful moment it was when
at last I took my little mother in my arms and bade her farewell! And it was just as difficult when later we said goodby to
our dear father. These tender memories I most assuredly will
never forget.

But now the break with home and family had finally been made.
With new appreciation we looked back upon that dear home where
we had spent so many happy hours with loved ones, and we hardly
dared to hope to see it again. Taking leave of relatives and friends
in Hudiksvall was not quite so painful.

On the morning of July 21 we boarded the steamer "Thule"
bound for the port city of Gefle and arrived there about five
o'clock that afternoon. We were compelled to lay over in Gefle
for three weeks waiting for our ship. During this time we were
quartered in a warehouse located on an island in the Gefle River,
which empties into the harbor. For several days I was sick, and to
make matters worse I suffered an acute attack of homesickness. I

was so miserable that I seriously thought about returning home again, but soon I felt better. Meanwhile there was much shopping to be done in Gefle since we had to provide our own supplies for the voyage. Finally, by August 17, our ship was ready to sail. We were permitted to come aboard with our baggage and supplies on the 15th; on the 16th everything was packed away and stored in its proper place, and on Saturday morning, August 17, 1850, the canvas was hoisted and we sailed out of Gefle Harbor.

We had a favorable wind all the way to Öregrund, where we anchored for the night. Sunday, August 18, was a cloudy day, and we sailed before a stronger breeze from Öregrund through the Sea of Åland, which is full of rocks and skerries. In the afternoon we sailed into the Baltic Sea. Now the ship began to roll and pitch, and we all soon learned what it means to be seasick. On the following day, August 19, the wind became still stronger, so that it was impossible to use any sails. Nearly everyone was seasick, and we lay in our bunks trying to do what we could to relieve one another during this unpleasant experience. This was a rugged day! The next day was even worse, and I was heartily sorry that I had ventured out on this journey, but it was now too late to turn back. In the afternoon of that day the first death on board our vessel occurred when the ship's carpenter fell from the foremast and was killed. He was undoubtedly drunk, but he had a wife and several children in Gefle who would certainly bemoan his fate. On August 21 a proper funeral service was held, and the remains were committed to the rolling waves. On the 22nd the wind was pleasant, and in the evening of the 23rd we had a thunder and hail storm. On the 24th we tacked toward Bornholm, an island belonging to Denmark. Because of contrary winds we cruised back and forth along the shores of Bornholm until August 30. During this time we had opportunity to get a good look at this island with its little city, Rönne. While we were thus cruising, the inhabitants of the island came out to us in small boats, offering to sell us various products, such as potatoes, fish, eggs, liquor, meat, etc. One morning during this time death again visited us as three small boys aboard our ship died, to be followed shortly by the death of a seven-year-old youth, all of whom were buried at sea, about two Swedish miles from Trelleborg, after proper funeral rites had been conducted on board ship.

On August 31 we sighted the northern coast of Rugen, and sailing past Denmark's capital city of Copenhagen we anchored at Helsingör on Sunday, September 1. The weather was fair, and by this time most of us had recovered from our seasickness. A beautiful panorama spread before us. The Swedish side of the sound is nearby, and directly across from Helsingör is the beautiful city of Helsingborg. In the harbor lay a whole flotilla of ships. Fort Kroneborg, located on a small island in the sound, stands guard over the strait so that no vessel may pass without paying toll. Our captain was obliged to pay a toll of thirteen hundred rix-dollars.

We remained here until September 6, when we again spread our sails before a favorable wind. Many vessels sailed from Helsingör at the same time we did, but we soon left them far behind. On September 6 and 7 we sailed up the Kattegat, and on September 8 we passed through the Skagerak, catching a glimpse the following day of Cape Lindesnäs, the southernmost tip of Norway.

We had fair weather and favorable winds across the North Sea. During the night of September 15 and 16 we entered the English Channel and saw Dover on the English coast, but we could not see anything of the French coast. The wind favored us all the way through the channel, and by September 17 we had reached the Bay of Biscay. The day following, September 18, we were out on the Atlantic Ocean. Here the wind blew stronger and somewhat contrary. On September 19 we sighted an immense school of porpoises.

On September 12 Olof Person, from Gässåsen parish, died.

When he had boarded the ship he was in the best of health but was suddenly taken ill with a raging fever on September 7. He had entertained high hopes for a bright future in America and often remarked, "When I get to America I am just going to sit around in the shade and do a little fishing and hunting to keep myself occupied." I hope he died a saved soul.

September 22, which fell on the Seventeenth Sunday after Trinity, brought us a strong side wind, but we still made better time than we had heretofore attained, the ship actually making a speed of eleven knots an hour. The following morning, the 23rd, it was clear, but in the afternoon we encountered contrary winds. The 24th was more of the same, but otherwise it was pleasant the entire day. September 25 found the wind blowing against us all day, and this continued for the next two days. On the 27th we saw a great many sea gulls. On the 28th a side wind began to blow, but on the 29th, which was St. Michael's Sunday, we had calm weather.

October 1 was a beautiful day with a brisk wind, but about 1 P.M. a sudden storm arose which continued until about midnight. October 2 was calm. October 3 was calm; in the evening, in the moonlight, we caught sight of a large whale which swam right up to our ship. This creature was a fearsome sight as he spouted great columns of water. The 4th was a beautiful day with a brisk side wind. On the 5th we encountered contrary winds, but for the next several days we had mostly favorable wind and good sailing. On the 10th we entered the gulf stream, and that evening, between ten and eleven o'clock, the cabin boy fell from the top of the main mast into the sea as he was trying to fasten the main sail. We heard him crying for help for about ten minutes, but it was pitch dark and the wind was strong, so there was nothing we could do to rescue him. In connection with this episode a near panic broke out on the ship because of an old woman from Gnarp. She was up stirring around when she heard the commotion among the sailors because of the man overboard. Without knowing what had happened, she looked up from the passenger hold and, seeing the reflection of lanterns on the wet deck of the ship, she thought the vessel was on fire. Scrambling back into the passenger hold she screamed: "Men! Fire! Fire! The boat is burning!" I and the other immigrants were asleep, but her screams awakened us, and throwing myself from my bunk I pulled on my pants as hurriedly as possible and climbed up on deck to find out what was going on. When I discovered that there was no fire but that one of the sailors had fallen overboard, my fears were changed to grief for the unfortunate victim of this accident at sea.

On October 11 we encountered contrary winds and the most violent storm we had yet experienced on the voyage. Huge waves pounded our little ship until we feared it would break into bits. This foul weather continued, almost without abatement, for three days. The morning of the 15th dawned clear and bright, and the temperature was so high that we had never felt such warmth even on midsummer day in Sweden. But about 9 A.M. the wind shifted and a gale arose which was so severe that we did not dare to walk about on deck for fear of being swept overboard. The next couple of days brought contrary winds and we made little progress. On the 18th we met another ship, which passed so near that the captains shouted greetings to each other. On the 20th, which was a beautiful day, the wife of Eric Westerlund died, and the following day she was buried at sea. Favorable winds and weather continued for several days. About dusk on the evening of the 23rd Olof Abrahamson, from Bergsjö, died, leaving behind his wife and four small children.

On October 26 we again entered the gulf stream and reckoned that we were now about six degrees from New York. This day marked my seventeenth birthday, and it rained all day. In the evening of the 27th the weather changed; a howling, cold wind arose which stayed with us for two days. During this time we saw several sailing ships at a distance. On the evening of the 29th a pilot came aboard our ship; he was the first human being from America we had laid eyes on, and he was indeed a most welcome sight. We had, of course, seen signs of land for several days, such as flocks of black birds and sea gulls, but the pilot was an even more definite sign that we were nearing our destination. We were very happy when he came aboard and spoke to us in English, even though none of us understood a word he said. The pilot boats from New York harbor are small sailing vessels, the finest, indeed, that can be found anywhere. They are of medium size with only one mast, but they are well made and sturdily fashioned. These boats can even cross the ocean.

On the night between October 30 and 31 we landed at Sandy Hook, about one and a half Swedish miles from New York, where we anchored until morning. After we had anchored a number of pilot boats came alongside offering to tow us into New York harbor. All manner of ocean vessels were anchored around us. At sunup our captain, Norberg, hired a steamboat to tow us in for thirty-five dollars. A tow line was attached to our ship and we were slowly hauled into port. Just as the boat started to move toward the harbor, the little daughter of Alfred Nord, who had been ill for several days, died, and her body was taken ashore by the inspector who came aboard to see if there were any passengers with infectious diseases in our company.

The scene on both sides of the entrance to New York Harbor is beautiful. Staten Island is filled with row upon row of small, neat houses, many of them of Gothic style. The harbor of New York is completed on the Long Island side, but is still under construction on the Staten Island side. Steamboats of all kinds chug here and there in the harbor. About three o'clock in the afternoon we drew ashore at the mouth of the Hudson River. Everywhere were countless ships and vessels of every kind and description from every part of the world, and the ship masts in the harbor resembled a veritable forest. We were deeply impressed as we surveyed the broad scene of a great city and its environs.

There was much commotion and noise on all sides, with hordes of people talking and yelling to one another, not a word of which we were able to understand. The moment our ship docked a crowd of people swarmed aboard, some anxious and eager to peddle various kinds of wares to the passengers, others to beg, and some to steal and pilfer if they found the right opportunity. There were several Swedish people among those who came aboard. They told us that there is a Swedish Methodist congregation in New York which uses a large ship in the harbor as its church. The vessel, called "Bethel Ship," is located near our dock and is furnished with all the necessary accommodations for a worshiping congregation. The pastor is Olof G. Hedstrom, a man of good will who seeks to do what he can on behalf of his fellowmen. He is an ardent episcopal Methodist.[11]

In the evening of the day we landed in New York, I, together with Jöns Per Anderson, Anders Ersson of Gnarp, Hans Smith, Anders Nord of Bergsjö, and others went to find the Rev. Olof Hedstrom on the "Bethel Ship," hoping to obtain his advice regarding our journey inland. We found him to be a very friendly man, and he counseled us in both practical and spiritual matters, but we noticed immediately his Methodist bias. He invited us to attend services on the "Bethel Ship," and the next evening we did so and heard him preach. During the sermon he gestured so violently with both arms and legs that we were actually dismayed; such preaching we had never before beheld. The following Sunday a number of our party received Holy Communion at Hedstrom's chapel, but

[11] Olof G. Hedstrom (1803-1877) and his brother Jonas (1813-1859) were among the early immigrants coming from Sweden to America in the nineteenth century. Olof arrived in 1826 and Joanas came in 1833. Both men left the Lutheran church and became Methodist evangelists, Olof in New York and Jonas in Illinois. Through their influence many Swedish immigrants were won for the Methodist church, and the main stream of Swedish immigration was directed to the Mississippi Valley.

I and a few others abstained. I asked Hedstrom about the possibilities of studying for the holy ministry, but he could give me no advice except that if I became a Methodist I could very likely find ways and means of entering the regular ministry. It seems that the Methodists take almost anyone into the ministry who can read and write a little, but this advice I was not ready to follow, so we parted company.

New York is a large, busy commercial city which with its great resources will undoubtedly some day become the largest metropolis in the world. It has a large number of imposing buildings, and the location is superb. There are navigable waters on three sides, while a supply of fresh water, drawn through large pipes from a lake out in the country, brings excellent drinking water to the entire community, although a few homes have their own private wells. There are many interesting sights to see and places to visit, but the time is short and we have much to do, so our sightseeing will be very limited.

On November 4 we contracted with a Swede in New York named Björkman, an agent for a transportation company who seemed to be a responsible individual, for passage to Chicago at the rate of eight dollars per person. Our baggage was taken on board a steamer, the "Isaac Newton," a large vessel with elegantly furnished cabins.

We left New York about six o'clock on the evening of November 4. Our entire party was on board except the following who remained in New York: O. Hammarström and his wife and two children; O. Hamrin, a painter from Attmar; Jöns Person from Åslund with his wife and infant daughter; and Britta Harm, a servant girl who deserted us as soon as we docked in New York. The reason she left us was that during the journey across the sea she got mixed up with the sailors on the ship, and when Per Anderson's Karin warned her, she became very angry and took her revenge by running away from us as soon as we landed.

We sailed up the Hudson River bound for Albany. Although we could not see much because of the darkness, we were able to discern enough to realize that we were passing through a very picturesque countryside. Though our boat was crowded with immigrant passengers who were tired and hungry, the night passed rather quickly, and we reached Albany just at daybreak. We hurried ashore and found a cafe where we had breakfast. In the meantime our baggage was being transferred from the boat to the railroad. We had carried an interpreter with us from New York, a Swede by the name of Pålson, a real rascal, who had no qualms about defrauding his own countrymen. When we were purchasing our tickets at the railroad station he tried to cheat us, but we caught him in his dishonesty and were reimbursed for the overcharge he had tried to get away with.

Albany, the capital of the state of New York, is a large and very busy city. A constant stream of ships ply the Hudson River between New York and Albany. About noon on November 5 we left Albany by train for Buffalo. We had hardly heard of a railroad, much less seen one, and we all wondered greatly about our trip by train. The coaches in which we rode had no conveniences, not even wooden seats, except lengthwise along the sides. We could sit or lie down on the floor, but this was not comfortable. A few minutes after we were on board the whole train of twenty cars, filled with people and baggage, started with a tremendous jolt. We proceeded slowly through the city and a little distance beyond, and then we began to climb through hill country. Now two engines had to be used, one in front and one behind. We continued thus for a while, but presently we reached more level terrain, one locomotive was detached, and our speed increased. Now and then the whole train would jerk and jolt as if it were being torn apart, and we would all be almost unbearably frightened. We passed through five rather large cities, namely, Schenectady, Utica, Syracuse, Rochester, and Attica as well as a number of smaller towns. The surrounding countryside seemed beautiful, with rich soil and varied topography.

On November 6, at two o'clock in the afternoon, we arrived in Buffalo in the midst of a cold and drizzling rain. We stood on the railroad platform huddled together like a flock of bewildered sheep, not knowing where to go to present our transportation contracts so that we could proceed with our journey. Fortunately, I was able to speak a little German, and when two somewhat respectable Germans approached, I spoke to them about our dilemma, and they told us to go downtown to the offices of the steamship company. So we started off toward town, trooping along like a flock of geese, drenched to the skin in the downpour of rain. There was a good deal of grumbling and complaining, and some wondered if we would ever survive our ordeals. To make things worse, Anders Ersson from Grängsjö parish lost his pregnant wife, and we had a frantic time running around looking for her.

After finding the office of the steamship company and arranging for our transportation, we began to look for lodgings for the night. Finally we ran across some Norwegians who helped us find rooms for our party. Several of our group stayed with a Mr. Larson, who owned a small store near the waterfront. Others, including myself, rented rooms from a German merchant in the neighborhood.

We stayed in Buffalo for two days, November 7 and 8, waiting for our boat. Late in the afternoon of the 8th we left Buffalo bound for Chicago, a journey which was very trying and difficult for all of us because our boat, the "Sultana," was a wretched, ramshackle, old hulk without comforts or conveniences. We had no rooms except the filthy, open deck, even though the weather was very cold. Both decks were crowded with disorderly Irishmen who behaved more like animals than human beings. Those of our party who had small children were compelled to rent the two available rooms on the upper decks for an extra payment of forty dollars, which they could ill afford. I and a few others who became ill during this trip shared these crowded quarters with them for a while. Because of my illness I was unable to see much of our surroundings. The water was rough and our boat pitched and rolled its way through the turbulent waves, and some days we saw no sign of land at all. On Sunday, November 9, our miserable boat ran aground on a sandbar in Lake St. Clair, between Lake Erie and Lake Huron. There we sat for half a day trying to get loose. Finally most of the passengers and almost all of the freight were transferred by means of a small steamer over to the Canadian side until our ship was finally freed toward evening, and people and baggage were brought back on board to continue our journey. Now and then we stopped at cities and villages on both sides of the lake. From Lake Michigan we caught glimpses of Wisconsin, a beautiful region apparently covered with a dense growth of pine forests.

Late in the afternoon of November 14 we arrived in Chicago, a large city located at the point where the Chicago River empties into Lake Michigan. Chicago is larger than the Swedish port of Gefle and nearly as big as Stockholm. It gives promise of becoming one of the biggest cities in the world. It lies on an absolutely level plain, and there are no hills or bluffs to be seen anywhere. There is a Swedish church and congregation located in the city which is served by the Rev. G. Unonius, who professes adherence to the high-churchly Episcopalian communion while at the same time declaring that he is also a genuine Lutheran, indeed, a true representative of the Swedish state church. There is also a Norwegian Lutheran church and congregation here of which the Rev. Paul Andersen is the minister.[12]

November 15 found us busily making preparations for our trip

---

[12] Gustaf Unonius (1810-1902) came to America in 1841, settling in Pine Lake, Wisconsin. Here he joined the Episcopal church and later was ordained into the Episcopal ministry. In 1849 he organized the first Swedish Episcopal church in Chicago. Paul Andersen (1821-1892) became one of the leaders in the organization of the Lutheran Augustana Synod in 1860.

to La Salle by canal boat.[13] The Rev. Mr. Unonius helped us get our tickets and make other arrangements for the journey. We hired an interpreter by the name of Per Ersson, who was to go with us to La Salle. Ersson, a native of Västmanland, seemed to be a responsible individual; he is a brother-in-law of Mr. Ruth, who shot and killed Eric Jansson.[14] Ersson had a neat little home near the Swedish church north of the river. We paid him ten dollars for his services. On this day, also, I sought the counsel of the Rev. Mr. Unonius regarding my studies. He advised me to continue on the journey with the rest of the immigrant party and requested me to send him my permanent address. He would then write and give me his considered judgment with reference to my schooling. I did not know at that time that Unonius was a member of the Episcopal church. I was therefore anxious to follow his advice and do as he told me.

The next morning, November 16, just as the canal boat was ready to leave the landing, an elderly Swede brought me a message from Mr. Unonius saying that he had decided that I could stay in Chicago. But it was now too late for that, since I could not get my baggage off the boat at the last minute. Surely this turned out to be a most providential circumstance. The only one of our party who remained in Chicago was the musician, Mr. Michaelson, from Attmar.

The tickets from Chicago to La Salle cost $2.75 per person. No sooner had we got under way than it began to snow, with a sharp drop in temperature. Our boat was overcrowded and had no conveniences; indeed, there was not even enough room for the passengers to lie down to sleep. Along the canal route the land was open and level, with groves of trees growing here and there along the way. We arrived in La Salle in the evening of November 19 but

---

[13] Via the Michigan-Illinois Canal which connects Lake Michigan and the Illinois River.

[14] On Eric Jansson, see below, p. 134, n. 13. Jansson's murder by John Ruth in the courthouse at Cambridge, Illinois, occurred May 13, 1850.

stayed on board the boat until next morning. La Salle and Peru are two insignificant little towns near the point where the canal enters the Illinois River, which in turn flows into the Mississippi River some distance north of the confluence of the Mississippi and Missouri rivers.

In the afternoon of November 20, H. Smith, my brother, and I, together with a number of others, leaving our baggage in La Salle, started walking toward Andover, some sixty or seventy miles distant. Those of our group who could afford to hire horses and wagons did not leave until the following day. When we had walked a few miles we began to feel weak and faint. We were not accustomed to this kind of activity because we had not walked any great distance since boarding ship in Sweden. Furthermore, we did not know the way to Andover and were unable to communicate with anyone who might direct us. Meanwhile it was getting dark, and we had no idea where we would spend the night. After some discussion we decided to camp overnight along the road, but we found the ground so wet and soggy that this plan had to be abandoned. There was no other alternative for us, a company of some fifteen people, including several small children, than to continue on our way. It was getting darker and darker, but after a while we came to an old dilapidated log house a short distance from the road. There were also farmhouses in the neighborhood, but when we asked about lodging for the night we were told that there was no room. Thus we were compelled to make use of the dilapidated old hut which would not have been considered even a decent cowshed back home in Sweden. The hut had two broken windows and a door which could not be closed. In the middle of the room stood an old stove, and alongside one wall we found several lengths of rusty stovepipe, but not enough to reach out through the roof. Nevertheless, we arranged things as well as we could. We gathered wood and cornstalks and soon had a fire going in the old stove so we could warm ourselves. Some of our party had a few potatoes, others some flour, and a few had cooking utensils. So we cooked some gruel of potatoes and flour, and this constituted our supper.

When we had finished our meal and were busily preparing for the night and discussing our present difficulties, a man with a gun and two big dogs suddenly burst into the room. He looked us over without saying a word, and we thought for sure that he was about to drive us out into the night, but to our grateful relief this did not occur. In a few moments the man turned his back on us and departed. We continued our preparations for the night by spreading leaves to cover the rotten floor. Soon we were all stretched out on the floor trying to catch a few winks of sleep. Next morning we arose early and prepared a simple breakfast of the same kind of gruel we had eaten in the evening, and then we set out again on our way to Andover.

Before we had traveled very far we were overtaken by the rest of our company who had hired horses and wagons to transport them to Andover. And what a wild ride they were having! The drivers turned out to be drunken, irresponsible ruffians who drove the horses at breakneck speed over the bumpy trails, and no one could say anything to them since they did not understand Swedish.

The wagons were piled high with trunks, boxes, and bags, and on top of them all the women and children and some of the older men were to sit, while the stronger ones were to walk or run alongside, trying their best to keep each load from tipping over. Some of those traveling on foot could not keep up with the speeding wagons, and so the group was split. Hans Smith and his family became so exhausted that they could not continue the journey. They stopped off at the home of a farmer, and I helped them to buy some milk. There were others, too, who were left behind. My brother and I, together with Anders Westerlund and Anders Wadlund, of Bergsjö, continued on our journey. Finally, we came to an open plain where we saw in the distance the small settlement of Princeton.

A short distance east of Princeton we came to a river. There was a bridge across the stream, and here an awful accident happened. Three of the drunken wagon drivers who had passed us earlier in the day had decided to race their rigs to see who could cross the narrow little bridge first. One of the wagons made it safely across, but one of the others was crowded off the approach and the load of goods and people tumbled into the river. When we came to the place we found that it was old Anders Westerlund, his wife Sarah, and two daughters who were involved in the accident. They had been sitting on top of the load, and when the wagon tipped over the old man had jumped and struck his head against the edge of the bridge with such force that he fractured his skull and was bleeding from both ears. At first he did not seem to realize the seriousness of his condition and had walked the rest of the way into Princeton, leaving to others the job of extricating the wagon and goods from the water. When we reached the bridge we helped to get the rig back on its wheels, loaded it again, and then made our way into the village of Princeton.

By the time we reached the town some of the wagons had gone on toward Andover, while others stayed there overnight. We found lodging with a Swede from Stockholm whose name was E. Wester, a barber and a man of real compassion for his countrymen. He gave us all possible aid. But now I discovered that the family of Hans Smith, who had been left behind, was not among us, and I realized that they would be worried and frightened out there alone on the prairie. Therefore I set out immediately to look for them, and about a mile and a half outside Princeton, to our mutual joy and relief, I met them on the road. The old man said to me, "You are a better man than I thought you were." It was pitch dark by the time I got back to town, accompanied by the Smith family. Since it was impossible to house our entire party in Mr. Wester's little barbershop, it was necessary to scour the neighborhood for additional night lodgings. By this time Mr. Westerlund, the injured man, was becoming desperately ill, and it was obvious to all of us that death was not far away.

We scurried everywhere seeking shelter for the night, but it was impossible to find rooms. It seemed to us that the villagers of Princeton heartlessly looked on us as if we were a herd of cattle. Finally we happened to meet a young Swedish farm hand, a native of Östergötland, who now worked for a minister about a mile and a half from town. He assured us that we would be permitted to spend the night in the minister's barn and that old man Westerlund and family could stay overnight in the minister's kitchen. Since there were no alternatives we gratefully accepted this offer. It was very cold, so we climbed up into the hayloft and crawled down into the hay to keep warm. It was a night I shall never forget, for men, women, and little children huddled together in the hayloft to find some shelter in this strange, new land of America. At the break of day we were to be up and out, but we were all so stiff from cold and exposure that it took some time before we could freely move around again. The Westerlunds spent the night in the kitchen, and there shortly after midnight the old man died, leaving his wife and children burdened with grief and care. The corpse had to be left there, and the minister was paid ten dollars for arranging the burial after our departure. I heard some time later that the driver of the wagon upon which Westerlund had been riding was arrested upon his return from Andover and on a warrant sworn out by Mr. Wester was brought to trial for his terrible deed. I do not know what was the final outcome of this sad experience.

When my brother and I crawled out of our shelter in the hayloft we walked into town and bought some bread, which we had for breakfast while we warmed ourselves by the stove in the store. Later in the morning my brother and I and a number of others left Princeton and continued our walk toward Andover, although we were suffering from sore feet and the cold weather. Others of our party decided to stay in Princeton, including Hans Smith, Olof Nilson, Anders Larson, Anders Nord, Olof Janson, Stephen Berglof, and Hans Kamal, together with their families. These people became the nucleus of the Swedish population in Princeton.

Those of us who were traveling on foot came to a place some distance from Princeton, where we bought some food and provisions at high prices. We were told that many of our people had stopped at this way station. Here, a few nights before, the wife of A. Ersson, from Gnarp, had given birth to a baby daughter, and as if this were not enough of a divine miracle, the next morning Mrs. Ersson climbed up on one of the wagons and with her little newborn babe in her arms rode over the rough and rugged trail all the way into Andover. As for us, we continued walking across the rolling prairies. By nightfall we came to a farmhouse where the farm family came out to meet us. By gestures and signs we made known our request for night lodgings and were permitted to bed down for the night on the bare kitchen floor. These were not luxurious accommodations, to be sure, but they were far better than those of the previous night. We were also provided with food for our supper, for which we paid very little. Our host lived about twenty miles from Andover in the vicinity of Bishop Hill.

The next day, November 23, we proceeded on our way in the midst of a cold and driving snowstorm. Late in the afternoon we arrived at Andover. We had expected to find at least a fair-sized village, but to our disappointment there were only a few scattered houses on the open prairie. Those who had hired wagons and teams were already on hand, and fortunately they had found the Rev. Mr. Esbjörn, who had helped them to settle with the troublesome drivers.[15] The tired travelers had found lodging with some of the Swedish families in Andover. Those of us who were traveling on foot stopped at a farm known as the Mix place, and there we found some members of our group. My brother and I found rooms in the home of H. Hasselius, a native of Ovansjö.

In the evening of November 24 I went to visit the Rev. Mr. Esbjörn, who lived about a mile and a half from where I was staying. When I got there I discovered that Anders Ersson, of Gnarp, and Jöns Per Anderson, of Hassela, had rented a room from Esbjörn and were lodging in his home. This was the first time I saw Esbjörn. He immediately impressed me as a kind, sympathetic, scholarly, and perhaps a somewhat stubborn person who had a real love for his flock but who was almost too dependent upon his wife. Having told him about my personal circumstances, I soon discovered that his opinions and advice were more nearly in agreement with my own viewpoint than any other with whom I had consulted. I was invited to stay for supper and after our evening meal I discussed my future with Esbjörn until late into the night.

I returned to my room, only to find that my brother had moved to other quarters. Though it was late at night I set out to find him, but lost my way in the darkness. Fortunately I stumbled upon the farmhouse of a Norwegian by the name of Smith, who permitted me to stay overnight. The next day, November 25, I returned to the Esbjörn home and was given permission to stay there for the time being. The same day my brother, together with several other young men, left Andover for the city of Galesburg, some twenty-five miles south, where he found temporary work as a farm hand. A short time later he returned to Andover and hired a rig to drive to La Salle for our baggage and belongings. His trip to La Salle

---

[15] Lars Paul Esbjörn (1808-1870) was the first minister of the Church of Sweden to lead an immigrant party to America in the nineteenth century. He arrived in 1849 and settled in Andover, Illinois. He led the movement for the founding of the Augustana Lutheran Synod and was the first president of Augustana Theological Seminary.

and return was without incident, and now we again had the few personal belongings we had brought with us from the homeland. We had now been in Andover for a whole month, and I was staying in the home of Esbjörn.

With Esbjörn in Andover

My stay in the Esbjörn home continued from November 25 to December 19, 1850. I did not desire to stay there any longer because Mrs. Esbjörn was troublesome and difficult to please, but for the sake of Esbjörn I would have been willing to stay. Regarding my own circumstances Esbjörn said: "Some time ago I received a letter from the Rev. Mr. Reynolds[16] in Columbus, Ohio, president of the Lutheran college there, informing me that the institution would be willing to support some young Swedish student who wants to prepare for the ministry, if I had any such student to send. But I wrote back saying that I knew of no one who could accept the offer. But now this opportunity is yours, and I advise you to accept it because it is the best you will find in the country and, moreover, the offer is extended by fellow Lutherans." I answered that since it was not at all certain what kind of Lutherans they were, I would postpone my decision for the time being. Nevertheless, Esbjörn wrote again to Reynolds, telling him that he now had a young man whom he could send to be trained for the ministerial calling. He even wrote to Dr. Passavant[17] in Pittsburgh asking him for money for my support. Passavant replied by sending twenty-two dollars.

On December 19 I left Andover and accompanied my brother to Galesburg. We arrived there in the evening, and I stayed overnight with a Swedish family. Many of the Galesburg Swedes are

[16] William M. Reynolds was president of Capital University, Columbus, Ohio, from 1850 to 1854.

[17] William A. Passavant (1821-1898), pastor, editor, and founder of the Lutheran female diaconate in America and of numerous Lutheran eleemosynary institutions throughout America.

Methodists. On December 20 a Swede named Renstedt went with me in search of a place for me to stay, but we were unsuccessful. The next day another Swede by the name of Swedberg accompanied me to the village of Knoxville, about four miles from Galesburg. He left me at the home of a Swedish shoemaker, where I stayed until noon the next day. The shoemaker and his family were good people, although they were Methodists. I was not able to find a job in Knoxville, so on December 22 I returned to Galesburg. The next day, which was Saturday, I found lodgings in the home of a Swedish tailor named Hedstrom, with whom I stayed until Monday, December 24. This day I met a student at the college in Galesburg, a Norwegian by the name of Andersen, a kind man and a brother of the Rev. Paul Andersen of Chicago. He did everything in his power to find me a place for the winter. Through his efforts I finally found a week's lodging with a farmer near Galesburg whose name was Hitchcock. Here I worked at various jobs, such as cutting wood and taking care of the farm animals, and on Christmas Day we even skinned a number of dead sheep, which seemed to me a singularly inappropriate job for Christmas. After my week with Mr. Hitchcock I looked up my brother, who had a job on another farm not too far away.

On Saturday, December 28, I stayed at the home of Mr. Renstedt, where I happened to meet Hans Smith, whom I had last seen in Princeton. He had come from Princeton in search of work and had stayed in Andover during Christmas. The Rev. Mr. Esbjörn had advised him to ask for work in Galesburg, but there were no jobs to be had. He found a place to stop at the home of the Swedish seaman John Youngberg, where he remained until Monday morning, December 30.

On Sunday the Methodist preacher Jonas Hedstrom conducted services in Galesburg in the home of the Swedish tailor Hedstrom, but Smith, my brother, and I did not attend. We stayed at Youngberg's and talked over our problems and discussed our circumstances.

At about eight o'clock on Monday morning Smith, my brother, and I left Galesburg for Andover. Walking across the prairie we came first to the little village of Henderson, about five miles north of Galesburg. It was a rugged walk in very cold weather. Late that evening we arrived again in Andover. Smith stayed with H. Nelson, who lived about a mile south of Esbjörn, and my brother and I went on to Eric Westerlund's home, which was situated next to the Esbjörn place.

December 31 was a bright and shining day, so I decided to walk to Rock Island and Moline to find a job and a place to live, because it was impossible to stay in Andover any longer, partly because of Mrs. Esbjörn and partly because of the limited possibilities for work. When I told Per Anderson, who had rented temporary quarters at the Esbjörn home, of my plans, he decided to go with me, for he found Andover impossible for the same reasons I did. Meanwhile we were joined by old man Smith, who intended to return to Princeton. He was very discouraged. He had no money and thus no way of getting his baggage and belongings from La Salle. His family had been living in a miserable shack in Princeton, sleeping on the bare floor since the middle of November, and there had been much sickness among them. They were in deplorable, and even desperate, circumstances. When Per Anderson now heard the old man's story, his good Christian heart was touched with compassion and he reached into his pocket and handed Smith a five-dollar gold piece, even though the old man already owed him more than three hundred rix-dollars which he had borrowed for the trip to America. This latest loan would enable the old man to get the family trunk from La Salle.

About ten o'clock in the forenoon we were at last ready to strike out for Rock Island and Moline. North of Andover, at a place called the Tavern, we parted company with H. Smith; he took a road leading southeast while we headed northwest. Per Anderson and I continued on our way across the broad prairies to the La Grange tavern, about six miles from Andover, and then on to Camden on the banks of the Rock River. Here, in the home of a respectable family, we secured loding for the night, for which we paid very little.

The next day, which was New Year's Day, January 1, 1851, we set out again for Rock Island, and about ten o'clock in the morning we arrived in Moline, having passed through Rock Island, which we found to be a rather sizable community. There were a number of Swedes who by this time had located in Moline. One of these was Jan Olsson, from Stenbo, who had bought a fine house for eight hundred dollars and in whose home we now found lodging. Olsson had been connected for a time with the Bishop Hill colony, but had left and moved to Moline. We visited with a number of our countrymen, and particularly with Carl Johanson, a tailor from Östergötland. He was a very friendly and congenial person and offered to help us in any way possible. Since there were many places for rent, we heard on every hand that it would be best for us to move to Moline. Therefore, on the following day we returned to Andover in order to make arrangements for the move. We arrived there in the evening, and I stayed with Per Anderson and his family until January 11, helping them to get ready to move. In the meantime the Rev. Mr. Esbjörn had received a reply from Dr. Passavant in Pittsburgh, enclosing twenty-two dollars for my keep in the Esbjörn home until I should leave for Columbus in the spring. Esbjörn was now adamant that I should stay with him, but I offered all kinds of excuses in order to get away.

On the morning of January 11 I left Andover, accompanied by Per Anderson's son Anders, and headed for Moline. We got as far as Camden that day, where we spent the night at the same place I had previously lodged. On Sunday, January 12, we proceeded to Rock Island, where we stopped at the home of Bäck and Lena Rolin. There we met several of our friends, including Jonas Norell, Peter Söderstrom, Jonas Ström, Eric Thomasson, and others. That afternoon for the first time we witnessed a Baptist baptism. The minister together with his congregation and many spectators stood on the shore of the Mississippi River, singing and reading Scripture. Then the minister took the candidate, an elderly man, by the hand and led him into the icy water up to his waist. Thereupon the minister immersed the man while he said, "I baptize you in the name of the Father, and the Son, and the Holy Spirit." While they waded ashore, another hymn was sung. There was no lingering on the river bank because everyone had to hurry home so as to avoid being frozen stiff.

On January 13 we went to Moline and I found lodging in the home of John Olsson. In the evening Per Anderson and his family arrived in town and found their way to the Olsson home. That was the same evening that the Rev. Jonas Hedstrom conducted services in the home of Olaus Bengston in Moline. I attended this affair, and it was the first time I heard Jonas Hedstrom preach. He took as his text a part of Romans 3, all of Romans 7, and a part of Romans 8. He turned this Scripture upside down and gave it, I am sorry to say, a bizarre and perverted interpretation.

The next day, January 14, Per Anderson and his family moved into a house which they rented from John Olsson. I stayed with them until the following Monday, and since I had no money, I was given free board and room by this kind family. On January 20 Mr. Carl Johanson, the tailor, promised that I could stay with him for the time being free of charge, so that I could do some studying and learn the English language. In the meantime I became acquainted with a middle-aged bachelor from Gnarp by the name of Abram Anderson. We agreed to rent a room together in the large house where Mr. Johanson lived, which belonged to a widow named Mrs. Bell. But the Lord had other plans for me.

One day as I sat studying my English grammar in the Johanson home, a farmer who lived some three miles west of Moline came to see Mr. Johanson on some business. After conversing a while with Mr. Johanson, and seeing me with my books, he asked about me. Presently he spoke to me, and with Mr. Johanson as interpreter, for I could not yet use the English language, he said: "Just come home with me and go to school. I will board you, and it will not cost you a cent for your instruction. Just work a little for me, as you can, and that will be all I will ask from you."

I accepted this invitation glady and went with him to his home, where I was kindly received by his wife and children. First, I attended school for five weeks and learned both to read and write English. After the close of the school term I worked on the farm for my board and room, studying between times. This family was very kind to me, and I was treated almost like one of the family. My benefactor's name was Abram Hartzel, a Pennsylvania Dutchman. He had six children, four boys and two girls. The oldest son, Cyrus, was fifteen years old, and the others were twelve, eight, and three; the oldest girl, Samantha, was fourteen years old, and her sister Amanda was six. Mr. Hartzel's neighbor was a farmer named Bromley, who had a very pretty daughter by the name of Anna Maria. She was fifteen years old, and a very fashionable young lady. The Hartzels were comfortably situated. Their large and beautiful farm was located about a mile west of the Rock River, between the river and a high bluff. They claimed to be Methodists, but were nevertheless respectable and God-fearing people. During the time I was there I often went to Moline to visit my friends and countrymen. Very frequently I was asked to write letters for my friends to their families and acquaintances in Sweden. On the morning of April 22, 1851, I took leave of my good friends, the Hartzel family. It was a difficult parting, for we all felt sad that our pleasant relationship must now end.

Journey to Columbus

On April 22 I was in Moline. I wrote a letter to Sweden for a young man from Östergötland, and for this I received fifty cents. That afternoon the Rev. Mr. Esbjörn and his son from Andover came to Moline, and in the evening we held religious services in a hall. Here I bade farewell to all my friends, who took up a collection for me which amounted to $3.60.[18]

The next day all preparations had been completed, and we were ready to take the first steamboat to Burlington, Iowa. In the evening, after a tearful farewell spent with my dear friends, the Johanson family, Esbjörn and I walked to the Moline boat landing. In the early morning hours of April 24 the S. S. "Lamartine" arrived, and we went on board, paying three dollars for our tickets. We left Moline, passing by Rock Island and Davenport, two rather attractive small cities. A little later we passed Fairfield, Muscatine, New Boston, and Oquaka, all of them small towns along the Mississippi.

We arrived at Burlington toward early evening and looked up some Swedish acquaintances of Esbjörn. We stayed overnight in the home of a Swede named Brydolph. Mr. Brydolph was the son of the pastor in Nerike, Sweden, and had been in this country for ten years. He had served in the army during the Mexican War[19] and was now working as a painter and decorator, a trade in which he was very capable. He was well educated and owned his own brick house, which was surrounded by a fine orchard. His wife was an English woman who had come from Illinois.

We spent the day of April 25 walking around town, taking in

---

[18] On Esbjörn's previous visits to Moline Norelius had been persuaded to accept the offer to enroll at Capital University in Columbus, Ohio. Esbjörn was accompanying young Norelius as far as Columbus, but would continue further eastward, visiting German and English Lutherans along the way, seeking financial help for the erection of church buildings for the Swedish immigrants in Illinois and Iowa.

[19] The war between the United States and Mexico, 1846-1848.

the sights. We visited a German minister named Dressel, who invited us to have dinner with him. He was pastor of a German Lutheran congregation in Burlington which had recently built a new church. Esbjörn was given permission to conduct Swedish services that evening in the basement of the new church. It was said that there were about two hundred Swedish settlers in the Burlington area at that time.

The next day, which was Saturday, April 26, Esbjörn made a trip to a Swedish settlement some forty miles northeast of Burlington. There he held divine worship the next day, while I preached in a schoolhouse located about four miles from town. I spent Monday, April 28, working in Mr. Brydolph's orchard. That evening there was a Masonic parade in Burlington in which Mr. Brydolph participated. On the 29th Esbjörn returned to Burlington, and that evening he administered Holy Communion to a congregation gathered in the schoolhouse where I had preached on Sunday. We stayed with Mr. Brydolph until May 4, waiting for a steamboat, and in the meantime I kept busy by working in our host's orchard.

On Sunday morning, May 4, the steamer "Danube" arrived in port, and we went aboard bound for St. Louis, Missouri, paying $3.50 each for our tickets. The next day, May 5, we landed in St. Louis about ten o'clock in the morning. Between Burlington and St. Louis we passed a number of small towns and cities, some of which were very attractively situated. One such place, called Cave in the Rock, was located at the foot of some high bluffs on the Illinois side of the river. In caves high up on the bluffs a band of robbers was said to have had its headquarters some years ago. These robbers plundered all traffic which plied up and down the river until officers of the law caught up with them. The Missouri River, which pours into the Mississippi some distance from St. Louis, is a very shallow stream, and its waters are very muddy, almost as thick as soup. At this point in the Mississippi there are shoals which require very skillful and careful navigation.

St. Louis is a large industrial city with good port facilities and many ships coming and going constantly. It is attractively situated. We were there only a few hours. At five o'clock in the afternoon we boarded another steamer, the S. S. "Genisee," bound for Cincinnati. Our tickets this time cost us six dollars each. Since leaving Burlington, there had been three persons in our party, including a young German lad named John Spielmann, who was also on his way to Columbus.

As we continued down the Mississippi we passed by many towns and cities, but few of them seemed to be of any considerable importance. The land along the river toward Cairo is, in general, low and level for approximately a mile on either side of the stream and then rises sharply in a series of steep bluffs. The high ground is usually covered with a dense growth of trees, and it is here that most of the towns and villages are situated.

During the night of May 6-7 we entered the Ohio River. South of us was Kentucky, and on the north Indiana. The Indiana shoreline was often lined with high, rocky cliffs, while the Kentucky shore was somewhat more level and covered with brush.

On the 7th we passed Evansville, Indiana, one of the most beautiful and important cities along our route. In the evening of the 8th we arrived at the falls in the Ohio River, just below the city of Louisville, where the river makes a bend toward the Indiana side. A canal three miles long takes the boat traffic past the falls, and this side trip requires several hours. We therefore left the boat and went on foot into the city, which is located at the upper end of the canal. Esbjörn had the address of two Swedish businessmen whom he had known in Sweden, and we set out to find them. It was a moonlit night, and it did not take long before we stood on the porch pounding on the door, since the residents had already retired for the night. One of the men was a Mr. Collin from Gefle, and the other was Mr. Ahlmark from Stockholm. We spent a pleasant hour visiting with these friends and their families, and about midnight we bade them farewell and returned again to our boat.

In the evening of May 9 we arrived at the port of Cincinnati, a large and busy city located in the southwest corner of the state of Ohio. The city is beautifully situated and is said to have the largest packing plant in the world. We stayed on the boat overnight, and the following morning, May 10, at about six o'clock, we boarded a train for Columbus. The fare was $2.50.

We arrived in Columbus about eleven o'clock that forenoon, and though I did not feel well most of the way, I was able to watch the passing landscape from our window. The state of Ohio is covered with a native forest growth, and the land is gently rolling. Among the numerous towns and villages we passed through was a city with the odd name of Xenia.

When we arrived in Columbus we set out immediately to find Dr. W. M. Reynolds, the president of Capital University. He lived on Friend Street in a moderately good, old-fashioned house. He was tall and slim and very obviously an educated person. We were invited to stay for dinner, and the Rev. Mr. Esbjörn had a long conversation with President Reynolds, with whom he had previously corresponded but whom he had never met personally. In the meantime, I became so ill that I had to go to bed in the Reynolds home. This was on Sunday. Toward the end of the week I had recovered sufficiently to move to a room on Green Street, which was to be my temporary quarters. Professor William Lehmann[20] visited me and informed me about the terms of my matriculation. My board, room, tuition, and two dollars per week would be provided by the Education Society of the school, while I was to furnish everything else, clothes, laundry, books, etc.,

[20] W. F. Lehmann (1820-1880) was professor at Capital University from 1846 to 1880.

and I was to repay the Society when my circumstances would permit. These arrangements were not entirely in accord with the promises made in letters to Esbjörn while we were in Illinois, and I began to wonder how I would get along here.

During the week I received some used clothing from Professor Essick.[21] For this I was very grateful since the clothes on my back were ragged, patched, and threadbare. By May 17 I had recovered my strength enough to move my few belongings to more permanent quarters in the residence of Judge Everhard. My board was to cost two dollars per week, and laundry privileges were to be twenty-five cents per week. I was so weak during this time, however, that I was unable to enroll in the school.

On May 19 Esbjörn, in company with several other ministers, left for a convention which was scheduled to meet in Canton, Ohio. From there he intended to go to Pittsburgh, then on to New York and Boston, accompanied by Dr. Reynolds. In Boston Esbjörn conferred with Miss Jenny Lind, who gave him fifteen hundred dollars for the erection of church buildings.[22] He continued his trip by way of Buffalo, Detroit, and Chicago. When he returned home again to Andover he had collected over two thousand dollars for new church buildings.

[21] A. Essick, a brother-in-law of William A. Reynolds, was a member of the faculty of Capital University from 1850 to 1854.

[22] Jenny Lind, the celebrated "Swedish Nightingale," was brought to America for a concert tour in 1851 by the famous entrepreneur P. T. Barnum. A deeply religious woman, she was distressed to learn of the destitution of her countrymen in America. In response to appeals for help Miss Lind gave identical gifts of fifteen hundred dollars to Capital University, Gustaf Unonius, and Lars Paul Esbjörn. On his eastern trip Esbjörn traveled about 3,600 miles, giving addresses at three different Lutheran synodical conventions which were then in session. Doors were opened to him in numerous congregations along the way, giving him opportunity to appeal for funds in Columbus, Pittsburgh, Philadelphia, New York, and elsewhere. Offerings were received and numerous private gifts were given. During this excursion Esbjörn collected about three thousand dollars in all. This money was the initial financial capital of the Swedish immigrant congregations and enabled them to erect their first church buildings in Andover and Moline, Illinois, and in New Sweden, Iowa.

2

STUDENT AT CAPITAL UNIVERSITY
1851-1853

On May 26 I started school and made very good progress during the first term, which began May 12 and concluded July 23. During this time I studied English grammar, geography, the *Fourth Reader,* spelling, and writing.

For the first three weeks of my stay in the Everhard residence I occupied a downstairs room alone. Thereafter I moved to a larger upstairs room, which I shared with two German theological students named Gratze and Schultze. The latter and his brother became my best friends. We spent many hours together, talking about religious matters, and found that our views were very similar. On July 6 I became ill again and did not attend classes for the rest of the school term, which ended July 23.

After the close of school I had to support myself as best I could. On account of my illness it was very difficult for me to earn money for the necessities I required. I was not strong enough to do heavy manual labor, and light work was almost impossible to find. Finally Dr. S. H. Smith, superintendent of the Lunatic Asylum, promised that I could come to him and do such work as I was able for my board and room.

On the morning of July 24 I went out to the Asylum, and along the way I met Dr. Smith, who was driving into town on some errand for the institution. He greeted me and told me to go to his office and wait there until he returned. I did as he said, and when he came back he put me to work at once trimming wallpaper. But he did not ask me a single question about my own circumstances—no, not a single word. The next day I worked in the library, cleaning and putting in order and making a catalogue of Dr. Smith's own books. Then I made copies of the Asylum's expense accounts for the years 1848 to 1851.

On the morning of August 5 I had to ask for more work to do and quite unintentionally said something that irritated Dr. Smith. He told me to carry up a pile of rubbish from the cellar, and since I did not clearly hear what he said I took my time in getting the job done. For this I received a harsh scolding. Although I finished what had been demanded of me, I thought to myself that to be asked to do this sort of menial work and then to receive abuse instead of good will more nearly befits a dumb dog than a student. The very next morning I packed my bag and after breakfast made my daily trip to the post office for the Asylum. Upon returning I went to Dr. Smith's office, thanked him for the privilege of staying there, picked up my luggage, and left the place.

Dr. Smith was a competent doctor, born and trained in England. Before coming to this country he had practiced medicine in Stockholm for ten years and therefore spoke fluent Swedish when he was so minded, but he was rarely inclined in this direction. His wife was of Swedish extraction, born and raised in Stockholm. Their son, Bernard, spoke excellent Swedish. The Smith household also included a Swedish maid from Stockholm. I felt that my relationship with Dr. Smith was rather strained, and it was obvious that life under such conditions is not very pleasant. Dr. Smith was, to be sure, an educated and cultured man. He was short and skinny, with grey-blue eyes and an unusually long nose.

On August 6 I went to Dr. Reynolds, and he put me to digging a ditch, for which I was paid a dollar. Then I went all over town trying to find work, but there were no jobs to be had. I spent the night in the home of Mr. Everhard. The next day, August 7, I went out on the streets again to look for work but found nothing suitable. So I thought to myself: "I am going out into the country and look for employment. Perhaps some farmer will have some work I can handle." Accordingly I ate my noonday meal at Everhard's, borrowed a knapsack from a fellow student by the name of Knauft, packed in a few clothes and some books, and started out. I headed straight north out of town, but had not gone far before it began to rain. Now the weather was as bleak and miserable as my own inner mood and spirit. Then I thought of the words of the Lord which remind us that "after the storm God sends the sunshine."[1]

After I had walked about four miles I came to a farmhouse, where I stopped and asked for work but was told that there were no odd jobs available. I continued on my way and after a while came to another farmhouse, where again I was turned away. A little farther down the road a third farmer gave me the same answer, and still farther on a fourth refusal. Finally, when it began to grow dark, I came to a small, low shack, where I hardly expected to find shelter but where I was permitted to spend the night. The people here were uneducated but were very hospitable and friendly. They charged me twelve cents for the night's lodging and breakfast.

I continued my trek northward next morning, August 8, and after going through a large forest I came to a farm in a clearing. When I asked the farmer if he could give me work for a few weeks, he replied, "If you can cut cordwood, you have a job." I said that I was unaccustomed to heavy work but that I would try my hand at cutting cordwood; if it proved too much I would have to quit. This seemed agreeable to the farmer, so I stayed there. The farmer and his family were respectable Irish Catholics. Their land

---

[1] Apparently an allusion to such passages as Ps. 107:28-29 and Mark 4:39.

was very level and nearly covered by dense woods. The farm lay some four miles north of Columbus. My first job was helping the farmer's sons to winnow wheat. I began cutting cordwood in the morning of my second day on the farm. But because it began to rain, I continued only for a half-day and was not able to lay up a full cord. Looking at my raw hands I realized that this work was too heavy for me, so I decided to quit and return to Columbus. That evening the sons were going into the marketplace with some produce and I accompanied them to the city. I told them that if I did not notify them by early morning the next day they would know that I had found other work and would not return home with them. In that event I would come back later and pick up some of my belongings which I had left at the farm.

As soon as I reached the city I went to the Everhard home and stayed there overnight. The next morning I sought out a book seller by the name of Mr. McHold. He gave me permission to try my hand at selling books on a commission basis. In the afternoon I started out with a medium load of books. I headed toward the southwest section of town and went from house to house, trying to peddle my books, but no one wanted to buy. By nightfall I had walked approximately ten miles and had sold one book for fifteen cents, on which my commission was five cents. Now I tried to find lodging for the night, but wherever I asked the answer was "no." Finally I found a place where I was permitted to sleep in the hayloft, so rather than spend the night under the open sky and on the bare ground, I crawled up into the barn and made my bed in the hay. When I awoke early the next morning I was so stiff and sore that I could hardly put one foot in front of the other. Nevertheless, I headed back toward Columbus.

This day, August 13, was my lucky day. Early in the forenoon I succeeded in selling a book for fifty cents, on which I earned a commission of ten cents. Then about half way to the city I was given a ride the rest of the way on a wagonload of wood. By

10:30 in the forenoon I was again at the Everhard home, where I rested in my room for the balance of the day. I secured a few days' work at Mr. Everhard's place. Meanwhile I also went out to the farm where I had left my belongings and brought them back to town. On August 18 Dr. Reynolds hired me to saw and split twenty-one cords of wood, a job which would last a good, long while. Here I could saw wood until I was tired, and then sit down and study my lessons. This was also the day when I received a letter from Eric Sandman, who lived near Farmersburgh in Clayton County, Iowa. He said that they had had a great deal of rain in Iowa this summer.

August 19 was uneventful. Nothing much to record in my diary. Continued to work on the woodpile. The same for the 20th, except that in the afternoon I sent a lengthy letter to my loved ones in Sweden. The postage cost me ten cents. This was the fourth letter I had written to my family since coming to America. The next several days were spent sawing wood and studying my lessons, with nothing of importance to record. On Sundays I usually attended the German and English Lutheran churches. One Sunday I also went to the Roman Catholic church, the largest church in Columbus. This was the first time I had ever been inside a Roman Catholic church. The Mass was conducted in Latin with organ accompaniment. The priest preached a sermon on Luke 18:9-15 but failed to give a single word of explanation regarding the text. Instead, he declared that God commands us to fulfill the law of righteousness, and if we fail we shall be condemned. In fact, it appeared to me as if he was trying to frighten people into love for God. Alas, that people should be so grievously misled!

September 8. I began my school work on this day. In the forenoon I had my first class in Greek and all went well. The afternoon was spent studying German and Greek. The following day was very much the same, except that in the evening I had a sore throat and felt a little feverish. Since I had no classes on September 10 I stayed at home and studied, even though I did not feel very well. My conscience bothered me lest I fall into the temptation of laziness, which so easily prevails when students live together. But the Lord Jesus sustained and strengthened me in all things.

On September 11 I awoke with a headache and a head cold but attended the class in Greek. All went very well. We are having unusually warm weather for this time of year. The Lord is gracious! The following day, September 12, I received some books from Professor Essick, a Greek grammar and a text on ancient geography. I must pay for these books out of my own pocket. At about one o'clock in the afternoon one of my professors, Mr. Tressler, died quite suddenly.[2] He was a young man, about twenty-six years old. Since he was inclined toward religious modernism it would be difficult to judge his spiritual condition. His passing serves to remind us that death is no respecter of persons or age. Classes were dismissed for the rest of the day. I spent some time reading and studying, and about seven o'clock in the evening called on a fellow student named Schultze, who introduced me to a new student, a German named Peter Eirich. This young man gave me the impression of being both proud and boastful. In fact, it seems to be characteristic of the German temperament that these people consider themselves just a little better than others and tend to boast and brag about themselves and their intellectual prowess. There are, of course, exceptions to this general rule among the Germans. O merciful Lord, help us to be truly humble, and be thou merciful to our limitations.

September 13 was unusually hot, dry, and dusty. The funeral for Professor Tressler was held in the afternoon, so we had no classes that day. In the forenoon a new student enrolled at school. His name is Solomon Schwingle. He became my roommate. That

[2] J. A. Tressler had been brought to Columbus from Gettysburg, Pa., by President Reynolds.

same day student Gratze, with whom I had roomed during the last semester, showed up at Everhard's asking for a room. Mr. Everhard did not like Gratze and said that all his rooms were taken. Poor Gratze was penniless and deeply in debt, but he had no one to whom he could turn for help so that he might continue his studies. I sympathized with him but with my limited means I could do nothing but pray for him. That evening I had a long talk with student Knauft concerning spiritual matters. He read the Bible and diligently sought more knowledge about life eternal but relied upon his own works and deeds as of some avail in winning God's favor. He believed that we can turn our hearts to God and cooperate with the Holy Spirit in our conversion. I tried to show him out of the Scriptures that we are entirely helpless to cooperate in our salvation but must wholly rely upon God's grace and mercy. He seemed to be attentive to my witness.

September 14, Thirteenth Sunday after Trinity. I stayed in my room during the forenoon and read Luther's *Postil* for the day as well as some other devotional writings. This day I felt an inner exaltation of spirit; I was glad and even light-hearted in Christ, who is my Lord and the Savior of the world. Such spiritual exaltation does not often fill the Christian's heart, even though he knows that he is secure in the blood of Christ and has peace in his conscience and with God. O heavenly Father, thy grace is great and abundant. Grant that we despise not this mercy which in thy love thou dost offer us!

In the evening I attended English worship in the Lutheran church nearby. A Jewish convert preached the sermon, using as his text Hebrews 2:3. Although he declared that salvation was full and free in Christ Jesus, he gave heavy emphasis to the law. He said very little about how a sinner may come just as he is to Christ. He was a short, little man with a dark complexion and black, curly hair. He had a good many mannerisms as he preached, some of which were not very pleasing. His manner of speaking was also somewhat distracting, since he would be shouting at the top of his voice one minute and the next would almost whisper so no one could hear him. He preached in both German and English. As far as I was concerned I must confess that his sermon was not entirely edifying, but I will not judge the man on the basis of a single sermon. Oh, how desirable it would be if the Jews would respond to the light of the gospel and be saved!

September 15 was a rather cool and refreshing day. I attended Greek class in the forenoon. My Greek class meets on Monday, Tuesday, Thursday, and Friday. The geography class meets on Wednesday. I do most of my studying by myself at home. It seems as if the Lord helps me study better when I am alone than when I try to study at school, surrounded by other students and subject to numerous restrictions and rules. In the evening student A. Schultze paid me a visit and we talked about both spiritual and temporal subjects. O Lord, enlighten my heart and mind! Illumine all people that they may see thy goodness and know that thou dost forgive every sinner who in penitence and faith confesses his sins before thee!

No classes were held at school from September 24 to 29 because the State Fair was held during this week in Columbus. On the morning of the 24th all the students and the entire family of Mr. Everhard went to the fair. The price of admission was twenty-five cents, but since I had no money I could not get in. Fortunately Mr. Everhard observed my predicament and gave me the price of admission. We arrived at the fair grounds about 9:30 in the morning, and the place was already crowded with people. A high fence of some six or eight feet in height enclosed the grounds, which stretch out almost a mile in length. The purpose of the fair is to encourage better and more efficient agriculture.

The entire grounds are furnished with display areas for produce and animals of all kinds, with walking space for spectators to view all the exhibits. The first creature I saw was a medium sized elk with a set of four-branched antlers. In another pen there were seven young elk calves. Further along the way I saw two beautiful deer. Toward the south end there was an exhibit of the most immense oxen I have ever beheld in all my life. Along the east side I saw many more exhibits of cattle, some of them with enormous horns. Opposite the cattle pens a long row of hog pens was arranged. Unbelievable though it sounds, I saw a hog as big as a good-sized bear. Next there was an almost innumerable collection of horses and mules of all sizes, colors, and descriptions. Some of the horses were exceptionally fine animals, and some of the mules were uncommonly ugly. One of the most interesting exhibits was in the poultry section—chickens, geese, and ducks of all kinds.

A special section of the fair was devoted to a large variety of machinery and transport vehicles. Some of these items were recent inventions. There were four separate exhibitions of such mechanical products. One of these, called the Florian Lounge, was decorated with the most beautiful floral exhibits I have ever seen. A number of beautiful young women, dressed in very becoming costumes, added much to the attractiveness of this exhibit.

Toward midday the judging of animals began. The object of this part of the program was to demonstrate how well bred and well developed the various types of horses and cattle were. There were two rings where the horses performed, and two for the cattle.

When I had walked around the entire fair grounds, I climbed up into the grandstand and sat down. Here I could get a good view of the tremendous crowds of people milling around below. I estimated that there must have been at least twenty thousand people there. And as I saw such a mass of humanity I felt strangely moved and thought to myself, "Will all these souls be saved? The answer is No." This was a distressing thought which wounded my spirit and awakened in me a deep sense of pity and concern for all those who do not know the one true God and him whom he has sent, even Jesus Christ, our Lord and Savior.

A little after two o'clock in the afternoon I left the fair grounds and arrived home about an hour later. I then went up to Broadway, about a mile north of the Everhard residence. It had been announced that a Mr. Vinning would make a balloon ascension on Broadway that afternoon, and I wanted to see this remarkable feat. About five o'clock the balloon went up. It was the biggest balloon I had ever seen, and I am sure it would have more than filled a good-sized Swedish hayloft. At first the big bag went straight up, but soon began drifting toward the northeast. It went higher and higher until finally it looked like a tiny speck in the sky. I watched for a while and then started back home. By this time I was tired and weary from the strenuous exertions of this unforgettable day.

September 27 was a cold, rainy day. Right after breakfast I practiced reading German with Mr. Schultze. After our German exercise we took a long walk through the woods about a half-mile from the Everhard residence. Later in the forenoon I called on Dr. Reynolds, but he was not at home and so I went to the post office. I received a letter from the Rev. Mr. Esbjörn, dated August 21, 1851. About four o'clock in the afternoon I returned to the Reynolds residence. Dr. Reynolds had returned home and we had a pleasant visit. He gave me ten dollars for some new clothing, since I was almost in rags. He also told me that there was a strong possibility that Jenny Lind, the great Swedish singer, would make a contribution to the school in Columbus, perhaps substantial enough to establish a Swedish professorship. Upon leaving Dr. Reynolds I went downtown and bought a new coat, a pair of pants, and a vest with the money I had received from him.

On October 10 I became ill and did not recover for almost a week. In the early morning hours of October 11 a big fire broke out in a slaughter house about a mile from my rooming house. I could see the towering flames from my window. In a short while the fire engines were brought up and the flames were soon under control. In the large cities of this country fire fighting is highly organized and efficient. Fire stations are located in various sections of the city, and in each section there is a big fire wagon with a very long tongue for pulling and equipped with a fire hose. Volunteers from the surrounding community are ready at all times to respond to a fire call. When a fire breaks out men come running to the fire station from all directions crying "Fire!" and soon there are enough gathered to pull the big wagon out of the station and up the street to the fire. Everything is so well organized and arranged that there is very little confusion; every man has a specific job to do, and soon the fire is under control. On every street there is a well or cistern which is kept full of water at all times. From such a reservoir the water is pumped to the burning building.

During this time I received a letter from Gustaf Palmquist, dated October 2, from Andover.[3] He had just arrived in Illinois from Sweden and had come to America for the purpose of preaching God's Word to his Swedish countrymen here. Because of my illness I was not able to reply to Palmquist's letter for several days.

October 14 was election day in Columbus. Both political parties, the Democrats and the Whigs, were very much in evidence. These are the two major political parties which seek office in the United States. The Whig party supports the policy of paper money, is friendly to the banks, and encourages domestic manufacturing. The Democrats say that they are opposed to all this. I must confess, however, that I am not yet well enough informed about American politics to see much difference between the Whigs and the Democrats. At some future time, when I have more information on the subject, I shall write more about this matter.

October 26. This day marks the anniversary of my birth. I could not help but feel deeply stirred when I considered that al-

---

[3] Gustaf Palmquist (1812-1867) left the Lutheran church and became a pioneer Baptist evangelist. He organized the first Swedish Baptist congregation in Rock Island, Illinois, in 1852.

mighty God determined just eighteen years ago to permit me to see the light of day, to let me have life from my mother's life in the early morning hours. I praise God for my physical birth, but even more for that spiritual birth which I received in Holy Baptism. Though I have often deserted my Lord, I heartily thank him that he has not abandoned me in my sin and condemned me to perdition but has drawn me to his bosom and given me grace to believe in him and to trust in him whom he has sent, even Jesus Christ. I thank thee, O God, for my Christian parents who raised me in the fear of the Lord. Grant them grace to remain faithful to thy Word and the faith which is active in love! Though I am far from my beloved parents, may it please thee, O Lord, to permit me to see them again in this life, for I would show them a double measure of honor and love. O Lord, my God, thou dost assuredly know the purpose for which thou hast created me. Make me competent to the fulfillment of thy purpose and content with thy will. Amen.

November 3. Today Jenny Lind arrived in Columbus to give a series of concerts. Everybody in the city is talking about her and making plans to hear her sing. This young woman is surely a Swedish nightingale.

November 4. This evening Jenny Lind gave her first concert here. Her singing has been received everywhere with the most astonishing enthusiasm. The following day Jenny Lind gave her second concert, her last appearance before returning to Sweden. I was most anxious to hear her but did not have money for the admission price. Jenny Lind is a native of Stockholm, Sweden, and is known as a mature and cultured woman. She is the world's foremost concert singer. Before leaving Columbus she contributed fifteen hundred dollars to our school for the purpose of establishing a Swedish professorship for the training of Swedish students at Capital University.

November 13. A cold and rainy day. This was the day I saw four American Indians, a man and three women, the first of this race I had seen since coming to America. They are not naturally ugly but they paint their faces in hideous colors. The women wore red woolen blankets in the manner that Swedish women sometimes wear long shawls. Their feet were shod in leather moccasins exactly like the Lapps in northern Sweden. Large silver earrings hung from their ears. They wore no hats but covered their heads with their blankets. They had black hair which hung in long braids. The Indian face is not full or large but formed rather like the face of the white man. The Indian man also wore a blanket but the color was blue. On his head he wore a bonnet of feathers almost like a crown. His cheeks were painted a light blue and the rest of his face a bright red, just like the women. All the Indians had piercing, black eyes, and in my estimation they were very similar to the Lapp people in the northern section of Scandinavia. The Indians went in and out of several stores and shops, apparently buying and selling. They spoke an Indian language which no one seemed to understand. They attracted a great deal of attention, and many people gathered to stare at them, which the Indians seemed to resent. A little while later I saw two more Indian men near the courthouse. They wore beautiful bonnets on their heads.

December 1. The days have gone by according to the usual routine. Good success has attended my school work, but I have made up my mind that next semester I will no longer attend classes but will undertake private study. This is in accordance with my own inclinations. I do not enjoy being a *scholasticus,* living under the constant jurisdiction and authority of others. I will perhaps attend the theological classes, but other studies I will pursue by myself.

December 3. Early this morning I went to the post office and received two letters. One was from Hans Smith and the other was from my brother Andrew, enclosing a letter from my family in Sweden. How happy I was to hear from them after waiting for a word from home for almost a whole year! When I read the letter from Sweden, however, I was filled with sadness. My parents have sold their homestead, the dear old home in Norrbäck, and have bought another farm in Torp parish, Medelpad. Oh, with what mingled feelings I received this news! I decided to write and beg them to come to America, promising to meet them in New York. For several days I was anxious and perturbed about my dear ones in Sweden, and I prayed earnestly that God would mercifully guide and direct our footsteps.

December 5. A cold and wintry day. Classes at school have gone well. I attended a meeting of the Theological Society, which convened in the school auditorium. Three of our students, Yetter, Strauss, and Worley, addressed the gathering on the subject, "Can the doctrine of the Trinity be adduced from the Old Testament?" It cannot be said, to be sure, that the presentations were heretical, but they were certainly not very edifying. Strauss, who is Jewish, has a splendid command of the Hebrew language. He was rather convincing in his arguments in favor of Old Testament evidence for the Trinity in opposition to the other two. For my part, whatever may or may not be the Old Testament evidence for the doctrine of the Trinity, I hold firmly to this Christian truth. The God who is the same yesterday, today, and forever, the Alpha and the Omega who has clearly revealed himself as the Triune God in the New Testament, is the same God who reveals himself in the Old Testament. It seems to me that the question itself is an error, since we hold not to one part of the Bible but to the entire Bible as the sure revelation of divine truth.

In this connection I must say that there seems to be little enough of genuine Christian faith in our Society—I mean the kind of faith which embraces Jesus Christ as Lord and Savior and relies upon his righteousness alone for the forgiveness of sins, life, and salvation. Such a real faith is not characteristic of our group here at school. But the fruits of unbelief are clearly evident among us, such as pride, anger, jealousy, hatred, etc.

December 9. The day dawned clear and bright, but before long it became very cloudy. Lessons at school went very well. I received a cordial letter from the Rev. L. P. Esbjörn enclosing ten dollars. He informed me that this splendid sum had been collected on my behalf by my many friends out west in Illinois to help me in the continuation of my school work. May the Lord bless every giver and help me to be a worthy recipient of such kindness.

December 17. This bitterly cold day marked the end of the school term. In the evening I read in the newspaper that Archbishop Wingård of Sweden had died at the age of seventy-one years and had bequeathed an estate estimated at $34,000 and a library of 15,000 books to Uppsala University. The library at Uppsala is said to contain at the present time some 288,000 volumes and more than 11,000 manuscripts. In the same newspaper I came across the information that there are currently 16,682 ministers in the United States and that they are paid an average salary per year of $375. I also noted that there are reported to be 16,000 prison inmates in this country as well as 217 institutions of higher learning. Another interesting bit of news states that Governor L. Kossuth of Hungary[4] has arrived for his second visit to this country. He has spent some time in England before coming here. He was enthusiastically received in New York. The purpose of the governor's visit is to seek the help of the United States in the attempt to make Hungary independent of Austrian rule.

December 18. A cold and wintry day with deep snow covering the ground. At nine o'clock in the morning I was at school for the beginning of the final term examinations. When the roll was called it was found that many students were absent. Professor Essick led us in prayer, after which we were given the examination in arithmetic, which did not turn out too well for me. Next the freshman class in Latin was examined. This went somewhat better.

---

[4] Louis Kossuth (1802-1894), leader of the Hungarian struggle for independence from Austria during the middle decades of the nineteenth century, was appointed provisional governor of Hungary, 1849. He visited England and the United States in 1851.

Finally the examination in geometry. In this subject some did well, others not so well. The next day examinations continued, and my first class was in geography, followed by examinations in Greek, English grammar, German, and chemistry. In the evening, after completing our examinations, the Brotherhood Society had a gathering with talks given by several students. Between the fall and winter semesters we have recess.

December 25. This is Christmas Day, the holy anniversary of our Savior's birth 1851 years ago. Here in America there is very slight observance of the Christmas holiday, but it ought not so to be. To be sure, in our motherland Christmas is also profaned, since there are many in Sweden who use the day only for play and worldly pleasure. When it is Christmas time such people think only of having a grand ball or something else sinful. I recall that last Christmas, which I spent near Galesburg, Illinois, I was skinning dead sheep. But I managed to celebrate Christmas by myself. For the right celebration of Christmas involves the heart and mind. It means being mindful of the purpose for which our Savior came to our world, which was to save our souls from eternal death. Now we should rejoice in God's abundant love and grace and thank him for his mercy, whether we are laboring or are in church on Christmas.

In the forenoon there was divine service in the German Lutheran church. Professor Lehmann[5] delivered a good sermon, as usual, after which Holy Communion was celebrated. This was done in a way that I had never before seen. The pastor first administered communion to himself. Then the men were served, standing before the altar, since there was no chancel railing. Finally the women received the sacrament. The words of institution were read when the bread and wine were distributed, but not for each individual communicant.

In the afternoon I attended divine worship in the English Lu-

[5] On Lehmann see above, p. 76, n. 20.

theran church where the Rev. Mr. Greenwald[6] preached a very good sermon on the text, "There is born unto you this day a Savior." The sermon was divided into two parts. The first part presented the little town of Bethlehem and the conditions prevailing there. The second part emphasized the great gift of Christ's incarnation. After the service I went home and spent the rest of the day writing letters.

December 31. This is the last day of the old year, 1851. Year after year hurries by, and many are called to their last resting place. May we all be mindful of the brevity of life on this earth and so prepare to enter that life which is eternal. I must confess that never before has time seemed so fleeting for me as it has during this eventful year. I began this year in Rock Island, Illinois, and now I will finish it in Columbus, Ohio. O Lord, my dear heavenly Father, help me to spend my time to thy honor and in thy service. Amen. Farewell, 1851!

The Second Year at Columbus

New Year 1852
Gone is the old year
The new is now here;
The Lord give his blessing
To all we hold dear.

January 1. The first day of the New Year began with a snowstorm and continued with cold and blustery weather. I spent the entire day reading good books, and my heart rejoiced within me. Here in America there are very few congregations which have special New Year's Day services. It is, rather, an occasion for fun and pleasure.

January 5. At nine o'clock this morning our class schedules at

[6] Emmanuel Greenwald (1811-1885) was pastor of the English Lutheran church in Columbus, Ohio, during Norelius' period of study at Capital University.

school resumed again. The courses which I took last term are being continued this term. I have worked during the afternoons very diligently with my Greek reader. I fear that I shall soon be immersed again in the whirl of school activities to the detriment of my own spiritual growth. I eagerly look forward to the time when I can quit these cloistered halls and turn my attention to more vital matters. To that end, my God, help and prosper me!

January 6. A big snowstorm. It began to snow the previous night and continued the following day until there was more than a foot of snow on the level ground, and here and there much deeper drifts. My Greek class met with Professor Essick at nine o'clock in the morning; the recitation went well. During the afternoon two of my roommates, Schwingle and Axeline, moved to their new quarters in the home of Mr. Bentz. Two other students took their place as my roommates; both are freshmen and seem to be somewhat stupid and slow. Mr. Crooks, who made his headquarters here since last September, returned this day from his travels and will stay with me for the time being.

January 25. A bright and cold Sunday. For the past several weeks the weather has been severe and temperatures often fall to zero and below. My school work has progressed satisfactorily and I have had no difficulty with my studies. On this Sunday I attended a service of Holy Communion and heard Professor Essick deliver an excellent sermon. I had not intended to go to Holy Communion this day since I had not attended the confessional service yesterday for certain personal reasons. But at the last moment I decided to commune without having attended public confession and in spite of satanic hindrances. I rest assured that I have truly and certainly received the body and blood of my Savior with the forgiveness of my sins. I have some difficulty in becoming accustomed to the manner in which the congregation here receives communion. I shall write further about this at some future time.

February 1. In the early morning hours, about three o'clock, fire broke out in the old courthouse in Columbus. About four o'clock I, together with several other students in our rooming house, ran through the streets until we reached the conflagration. Just as we got there flames enveloped the high steeple, and it began to topple. The firefighters stood helplessly by as the fire raged out of control. As I stood and watched the fire, I noted a real phenomenon, namely, that when the fire first broke out it was calm, and practically no wind was blowing. But within a short while a stiff breeze arose and whipped the fire into a raging inferno. This was certainly the devil's own work, for as usual, whenever trouble arises, he is there to make matters much worse. When I left the scene the fire was burning in full force. Because of the loss of sleep, I was heavy and dull in my head all the rest of the day. In the evening I went to church and heard a good sermon, but it was not the kind of preaching that converts people to Christianity.

February 4. At about six o'clock in the evening the famed Hungarian ex-governor and revolutionary, Louis Kossuth, arrived here in Columbus en route from Cleveland by train. He has come to America in order to awaken sympathy for the oppressed Hungarians and to collect financial aid for the support and continuation of the revolution in his homeland against the tyranny of Austria. He is a great man who seems to have a very worthy goal in mind. His arrival in Columbus caused a tremendous stir. He was met at the station by the mayor and a military platoon and escorted by brass bands and a great crowd of people to the Neil House, where he established his headquarters. In a few moments he appeared on the hotel balcony and greeted the huge crowd with these words: "Good evening, ladies and gentlemen! I see by the preparations you have made that you wish to receive me in a kind and gracious manner. Let me assure you that I am glad to be here as your guest. Since it is so late in the day, I will postpone my address to you until tomorrow morning at eleven o'clock. I have not yet had my dinner and am therefore hungry. So I bid you all a cordial goodnight." This speech was greeted with loud and long applause.

Next day, February 5, I attended my nine o'clock class at school and then went downtown to hear Governor Kossuth speak. A high speaker's platform had been erected in the open court in front of the State House. From this place he addressed thousands of people who had assembled to hear him at eleven o'clock in the forenoon.

A Presbyterian minister opened the meeting with prayer, which I felt was not quite suitable for such an occasion. Then a prominent lawyer from Ohio by the name of Galloway gave an excellent introduction to Mr. Kossuth. Now the great man himself stepped forward and, taking off his hat, politely acknowledged the introduction as the crowd cheered. He then put his hat back on his head because of the cold weather and began his address. His speech was in reality an expression of gratitude to the people of Ohio for their sympathy with and support of the Hungarian people. It was a short but very powerful address. His use of the English language was good, even though he occasionally mispronounced a word here and there. He was of medium build, had a heavy black beard and mustache, black hair, large blue eyes, and a light complexion. He wore a long overcoat, which was open and revealed a fine black satin frock coat embroidered with gold braid. Around the waist the speaker had a heavy gold chain, to which a sword was attached. A beautiful ostrich plume adorned his big black hat. He spoke with a resonant, deep voice which could easily be heard at a distance. He made a profound impression upon me, and I felt a sincere sympathy for the cause for which he was appealing. After his short address he returned to the Neil House and the ceremony was concluded. I returned home about noon. The stirring events of the forenoon made study in the afternoon very difficult, and by the end of the day I had accomplished very little.

February 8, Sunday. This day dawned clear and bright, a beautiful spring-like morning, and I awoke feeling unusually well and happy. As I beheld the beautiful day my thoughts turned to my old home in Sweden. I recalled with deepest nostalgia how joyous and beautiful it was when springtime came, and in my thoughts I again found my way up into the mountains, whose peaks were lifted high above the streams and valleys. O home, sweet home! Will I ever again lay eyes upon you? I attended church services this morning at which the Rev. Mr. Greenwald preached about Peter's denial. The sermon was fair but did not really come to grips with the message of the text, which has to do with the need for penitent faith in man's heart.

February 12. Partly cloudy, and the snow which had fallen the day before was almost completely melted. This was the day I started to tutor Dr. Reynolds in the use of the Swedish language. He reads well enough, but his pronunciation is frequently incorrect. It is a strange experience to act as the teacher of my professor.

February 24. At daybreak it was cloudy and threatening, but in a few hours the sun was shining, and my spirits were revived. Since I had no classes to attend I went to a wooded area about a mile and a half from town. There I was all alone, and as I walked through the woods I practiced public speaking by preaching to the trees. This is an excellent way to become an effective public speaker. After this exercise I continued to wander through the woods beholding the wondrous beauty of God's creation until it was time to return to my rooming house.

March 1. This evening I attended a lecture at the medical college in Columbus which was given by a Dr. Boient, of New York, on the subject of geology. He discussed various geological problems, and especially the phenomenon of various reptile fossils which are to be found in great numbers in the coal deposits of this hemisphere. The lecture was illustrated with a number of paintings and drawings. It is apparent that Dr. Boient is a very learned man who has traveled widely throughout the world. He had an attractive face and very long hair. The admission price for this lecture was ten cents.

March 11. An unusually mild day. I made inquiries about a new rooming house for next semester and succeeded in finding new quarters in the home of Mr. La Zalle. In the evening I attended a convocation held in the New School Presbyterian church for the benefit of Capital University. The audience was earnestly urged to give generously to the building fund of the school because the school can be of great service to the entire community. Judge Stone was asked to preside at the meeting. President Reynolds gave a historical sketch of the institution since its founding in 1850.[7] Attorney Dennison then gave a speech and proposed that a resolution commending the school to the public should be adopted. Thereupon attorney Galloway gave an inspiring address emphasizing the need for a good school in the city. Several pastors also arose and added their sentiments in favor of the institution. Having adopted the resolution calling for public support of the school the meeting was adjourned.

March 27. We have a week of recess between the winter and spring semesters at school. Mr. La Zalle hauled my belongings over to his place today, but I stayed at Everhard's until evening, when I went out to my new quarters. I had lived for the past ten months with the Everhard family and have looked upon this home as my own; it was therefore somewhat difficult for me to leave these familiar surroundings. I am sure, however, that I will enjoy my new quarters, and in any event it will be cheaper than living downtown.

[7] The Theological Seminary of the Evangelical Lutheran Joint Synod of Ohio and Other States was founded in 1830. In 1850 a "complete university after the European style" was established, of which the Theological Seminary was one department. See C. V. Sheatsley, *History of the First Lutheran Seminary of the West* (Columbus, O.: Lutheran Book Concern, 1930), pp. 39 f.; also D. B. Owens (ed.), *These Hundred Years: A Centennial History of Capital University* (Columbus: Capital University, 1955).

May 1. On this first day of May the weather was sunny and bright, but with a stiff breeze blowing. After class at school I went up to the city library to see what kind of place it was. It is a large and imposing institution. Anyone can go there and read without paying a fee. I think I shall spend my leisure hours at the public library. After lunch I read my Greek *Anabasis* for a while and then went to visit with Dr. Leuthstrom, who practices Swedish massage and homeopathy here in Columbus. I asked him to lend me four dollars, but he said that he did not have the money at the moment but would be able to help me within a week. I hope, however, that I will not need to avail myself of his generosity. Thereupon I went to see Dr. Reynolds. On the way I met Professor Essick, who gave me an old coat which fits me much better than the old frock coat he gave me a year ago. May the Lord bless him for his kindness to me.

For some time now I have been worried about my circumstances here at school. It has been my misfortune to fall into debt to the Education Society,[8] and this indebtedness, which amounts to about one hundred dollars, so occupies my mind that it hinders my studies. I am constantly thinking about ways and means of getting out of debt, but there seems to be no way out, no means of earning my way free and no person to whom I can turn for help. To be sure, my room and board are paid by the Education Society, but I have practically nothing to wear! I need clothes. And I need books and other supplies. Where shall all this come from? Furthermore, I am deeply concerned about my brother Andrew. His future does not seem very promising. And, finally, the uncertainties regarding my family and loved ones home in Sweden disturbs me, and I wonder how they are getting along and what they are planning for the future. Indeed, there is much about which to be anxious, but I must cast my cares and troubles upon the Lord in the confident hope that with him there is abundant help.

[8] A fund established at this school to give financial aid to needy students.

May 5. What a beautiful day! There were no classes at school, so I spent the afternoon with Clinton La Zalle, his sister, and another girl visiting here from Connecticut. We had a very pleasant time walking in the garden and through the woods, singing, conversing, and reading poetry. The time went too fast.

June 30. On this day the cornerstone was laid for Capital University's new building in Gooddale Park, where a large tract of land has been given to the school by Mr. Gooddale. At 3:30 in the afternoon Mr. La Zalle and I went downtown to the McHold's music store, where the band and the students were gathering for the parade to Gooddale Park. About an hour later the professors joined us. Mr. Schwingle, the tallest student in school, was chosen as the marshal of the parade. With the band heading the procession, our line of march took us first past the State House, where a large crowd joined the parade. Then with the band playing and the flags waving we marched up Broadway Avenue, and then turned west on Front Street and out to Gooddale Park and the new college site. The ceremonies began with Dr. Reynolds' placing various documents and other items in the cornerstone of the new building. These included a brief historical sketch of the school, a record attesting to the fact that the cornerstone was being laid at 5 P.M., June 30, A.D. 1852, when Lincoln Gooddale was chairman of the Board of Trustees and Dr. Reynolds was president of the institution, with the faculty consisting of Professors Lehmann, Essick, Wormley, and Worley, when the governor of the State of Ohio was the Honorable Mr. Wood and Millard Fillmore was President of the United States. In addition, copies of the school catalogue, the seminary constitution, the constitution of the State of Ohio, and several other documents were placed in the cornerstone. Thereupon the entire assembly sang a hymn. A short prayer was given by Pastor Greenwald, and then Mr. Galloway spoke briefly to the assembly. This was followed by a speech by Dr. Reynolds, and then Professor Lehmann said a few words in German. All these remarks were intended to encourage the people to give their warmest support to the school. Two other noted speakers were scheduled to appear but were unable to attend, and the crowd was obviously very disappointed. As a result a good many left the premises before the close of the ceremonies. It would seem that for such an important occasion more careful planning would be very desirable. After the close of the exercises I returned home and remained there for the rest of the day.

July 3. Tomorrow is Sunday, and therefore Independence Day is being celebrated today. It is not much of a celebration. About five o'clock in the evening there was a balloon ascension by a Mr. Weise. This is the third time I have seen this man go up in a balloon here in Columbus. It is quite a sight! The balloon is about eight feet in diameter and made of silk. It went up so high that it could not be seen with the naked eye. Nothing else of real interest occurred in connection with the celebration. I became acquainted this day with a fellow countryman by the name of Rystedt, from Östergötland. He seemed to be a very respectable fellow. He has been in this country only a short while and therefore does not speak English very fluently, but he will soon learn. After I returned home, Clinton La Zalle and I walked in the woods until it was dark.

July 7. This evening about seven o'clock an express train bearing the body of U. S. Senator Henry Clay came to Columbus from Cleveland, en route to Mr. Clay's home in Kentucky. Mr. Clay has been one of the most prominent members of the U. S. Senate and a noted orator. He died in Washington July 1, 1852. His parents were poor in worldly goods, and the father died when Henry was a small boy. The senator rose to prominence by reason of his own hard and disciplined labor. General Lewis Cass and Commodore Robert Field Stockton accompanied the body on this last trip home. An honor guard, together with a great crowd of people, formed at the depot and escorted the casket into the city. The marching guards in their uniforms, the stately band music, and the thunder of cannons saluting the national hero—all made a deep impression upon all of us. The body was brought to the State House to lie in state overnight, and thereupon the procession continued to the Neil House, where it dispersed.

July 14. I worked hard all day. A very sad letter reached me on this day. It was from my friend Gustaf Palmquist, informing me that he intends to forsake the Lutheran church of his fathers and become a Baptist. What a tragedy! Satan is surely busy with all his power and wiles, seeking to lure people from true faith and the gospel. These friends, with Wiberg and Palmquist in the front ranks, forsake our Evangelical Lutheran Church and cast themselves adrift on the uncertain ship of the Baptists. May a gracious God nevertheless save these friends by his mercy and rescue them finally from their errors. I now stand here bereft of my friends in faith and shed bitter tears over their apostasy!

July 28. The past several days I have been kept busy guarding Mr. La Zalle's apple orchard against thieves. Today I began cutting a field of oats with a scythe, but was often interrupted by apple thieves. A letter from the Rev. Mr. Esbjörn has arrived, bearing the melancholy tidings about his many trials and tribulations. On July 18 his beloved wife died in childbirth, but the infant, a girl, survives. Esbjörn was deeply devoted to his wife, even though in my opinion she was not exactly suited for him. He is certain that she died in peace with God through faith in Christ. In addition to this great bereavement Esbjörn has endured many other trials and burdens. May the Lord mercifully sustain and comfort him. Other letters which have reached me during the last few days have come from my brother, Andrew, and from Hans Smith. I am glad and thankful that at least some of my acquaintances are not converting to the Baptist faith.

August 1. On this Eighth Sunday after Trinity I was at home all day long guarding the orchard. The day was not entirely lost, however, since I had opportunity to spend some time reading my Greek New Testament. New light has dawned for me this day regarding the necessity and divine origin of baptism. I have discovered that the Greek verb *matheteuō* means "to make a disciple" and that *baptizontes,* the present participle of *baptizō,* indicates the method or mode through which one becomes a disciple. Praise God for this illumination! The past few days have been unusually cold and chilly for this time of year. We have had a good many visits from apple thieves today, but they have all been driven off the premises.

August 14. This afternoon I went to see my first carnival here in Columbus. The most interesting part was the menagerie of animals, and especially the elephant. I had never before seen an elephant. He was an extremely huge and clumsy brute, just like I had always imagined an elephant to be. What a sight! He was hairless but had an incredibly large head with a fantastically long nose and big teeth. His legs were thick as tree stumps, and his eyes small as pebbles. His ears were enormous but his tail was quite short. His long nose is used as a sort of arm and hand, so that the animal is very useful for many kinds of heavy work.

In contrast to the elephant there was a rhinoceros, who is practically useless but is nevertheless a remarkable beast. He, too, is indescribably clumsy, hairless, and huge. He is also very ugly. His tiny eyes sit far down on his nose. There was a horn on the end of his big nose, but the sharp end of the horn had been broken off.

There were also a number of lions on display. They were not quite so large as I had imagined lions to be, not nearly so large as a yearling colt. They have well-formed bodies, and as they paced to and fro in their cages they frequently let out the most awful roar. I also saw a number of tigers. These were somewhat smaller than the lions but almost as long. They were yellow with black stripes. They had large heads and looked very wild and ferocious. One of the tigers was entirely black. There was also a brown bear which was much larger than the lions but not so well proportioned. Other animals in the exhibition included leopards, anteaters, monkeys, etc. There was also a zebra, a queer looking creature belonging to some species of the horse family. It is a beautiful animal with black and white stripes over its sleek body. Then there was an ostrich, which was a good deal larger than I had imagined. When this bird stretched out its neck, it was from top to bottom almost twice as tall as I am. His head, neck, and legs were almost grotesque, and black feathers covered most of his body. There were also parrots and other strange creatures to which I paid less attention.

In addition to the animals, there were acrobats who performed some remarkable feats. One of the most outstanding was a rider who was the best I have ever seen. I spent two hours in the carnival, which cost me twenty-five cents for admission. After leaving the carnival I went downtown and met some friends. This was an eventful day.

September 1. The new school term began this day. There are only a few students on hand as yet. It takes some time to get the whole program going again. For myself, I am ready to begin my studies once more; I feel refreshed and eager to continue my schooling. May God help and bless me in these endeavors. After registering for new classes I chanced to meet my friend and countryman, Mr. Rystedt, and enjoyed visiting with him for a while.

September 8. School work is going well. In the afternoon I attended a Whig convention in Gooddale Park in Columbus. Senator Ewing, editor Horace Greeley, and a Dr. Rudby addressed the assembly, and I felt that their speeches were good and reasonable. I am becoming increasingly convinced that the Whig party offers the country the best political platform for the future, for it seeks to help and improve both manufacturing and agriculture. There is a good deal of excitement among the people regarding the coming presidential election. General Scott, the great war hero, is the

Whig candidate, while Franklin Pierce, who is known neither in military nor in political circles, is the Democratic candidate.

September 10. A very cloudy and gloomy day. Our chemistry class, with Dr. Wormley as our teacher, met for the first time this day. Professor Wormley, a medical doctor, seems to be a very capable chemist, and very careful and precise in his teaching methods. In the evening our so-called Smithsonian Fellowship, a theological society of which I am a member, held its first meeting of the new school year. There were not many present. Mr. Eirich gave a talk in English which was then the subject for discussion and criticism. Other matters were given consideration, and I did not get home until ten o'clock at night.

September 25. I am suffering from a miserable cold in the head. One of the class sessions this forenoon was devoted to a debate on the question, "Are the gold strikes in California and Australia a benefit to mankind?" Mr. Schwartz and I upheld the negative side and students Byerly and Melanchthon Everhard argued in favor of the positive side of the question. The debate went very well. The weather is improving.

October 7. The weather is clear and school work is progressing satisfactorily. At seven o'clock this evening I attended a lecture given by an elderly missionary representing the American Missionary Board. His name is Gooddale, and he has spent the past twenty-one years as a Christian missionary in Turkey. He has suffered many hardships on many occasions for the sake of the gospel and now seems to be a worn, old man. I found the lecture most interesting.

October 11. This has been a cold and clear day; school work progresses very well. We had our first lecture in Xenophon's *Memorabilia of Socrates* this forenoon. I have become enamored with Socratic philosophy, which seems to be singularly helpful and clear. A letter from my brother arrived this day. Andrew has informed me that he has gone over to the Baptist heresy. This grieves me very deeply. He has taken this regrettable step in ignorance, for I am sure that if he was able to read the New Testament in the original Greek, so as to understand the text, he would never have permitted himself to be deceived. I leave this melancholy situation in thy hands, O Lord! I pray that in thy mercy thou shalt illumine my dear brother regarding thy Word and truth. Lead thou all things to a blessed conclusion.

October 24. A beautiful Sunday. I attended divine service in church today and heard Dr. Reynolds preach a sermon on the subject, "All men must die." His text was Isaiah 64:6. The sermon was occasioned by the unexpected death of the Honorable Daniel Webster, of Massachusetts, one of America's greatest statesmen. He was known as the country's finest orator, at least as good as Patrick Henry or Henry Clay. He has been secretary of state for many years, an office which he occupied at the time of his death. The American people will sorely miss him. He was sixty-eight years old at the time of his sudden and unexpected passing. He had been urged to accept the presidential nomination but had refused this high honor.

October 26. And now another October 26! How fleeting the years! This day is now the nineteenth anniversary of my birth into this world. I thank thee, my heavenly Father, through Jesus Christ my Lord, that thou hast given me the gift of life. I thank thee for my Christian parents, my godly home and pious upbringing. I thank thee for my Swedish heritage; I am envious of no other. I thank thee for thy guiding and protecting mercy unto this very moment. I pray thee to lead and guide my footsteps in accordance with thy holy will. Grant me the gift of thy Holy Spirit that I may daily grow in thy favor and in right understanding. Help me that I do not become a mere hireling, but an earnest and honest laborer in thy kingdom. Bless and reward, O God, my beloved parents for their loving care for me, and if it be in accordance with thy will, permit me to see them again in this life on earth.

But above all else, let us all meet together in thy holy presence, in our heavenly home, together with all thy saved people, when our journey here on earth is finished. Forgive all my sins, and bestow upon me thy mercy and grace in the days that may lie ahead. And when my last hour shall finally come, stand by my side, O Lord, and lead me safely across the dark sea of death, in the name of the Father, the Son, and the Holy Spirit. Amen.

The past year has been very good to me. Although there have been some trials and tribulations, the joys and blessings have been far greater. I have made excellent progress in my academic studies during this year and have learned how to manage my affairs much more efficiently than was the case a year ago. On this my birthday I wish my dear parents and family back home every blessing and joy.

November 2. This is election day, when the entire population of the land which is of voting age goes to the polls and casts the ballot for the office of President of the United States. General Scott is the Whig candidate and Mr. Pierce represents the Democrats. Here in Columbus it has rained almost the whole day.

November 9. The Clionian Literary Society of our school held its monthly meeting this afternoon. I introduced a debate on the question, "Is universal suffrage of white male citizens of twenty-one years of age expedient?" I upheld the negative side, basing my argument on the principle that ignorance and inexperience cannot be depended upon for responsible action.

November 25. The government has designated this day as Thanksgiving Day. It is regrettable, however, that the majority of people pay very little attention to this holiday. Such indifference, it seems to me, is a downright vice, since failure to acknowledge God's great goodness and grace reflects a spirit of ungodliness and gross ingratitude. I attended service at our church and listened to an edifying sermon by Professor Essick. Part of the evening was spent tutoring my friend Mr. Rystedt in English.

December 2. This afternoon I attended a surprise party for the Rev. Mr. Greenwald. A large number of the members of the Lutheran congregation were there. The women of the church had made all the arrangements and invited the entire congregation to this festive occasion, the purpose of which was to encourage and express appreciation to Greenwald. He received a number of useful gifts from his many friends.

December 16. This has been a cold and stormy day. This evening I attended a meeting of the Clionian Society. The program consisted of a general discussion, which became almost too heated before it was concluded. As a society we decided to wear a black armband for the next thirty days as a sign of mourning for the death of our dear fellow member, student Henry Stanberg.

December 21. On this Sunday I attended divine service at our church and heard Dr. Reynolds preach. His sermon was well conceived but poorly delivered. That man is no public speaker! In the afternoon Mr. Rystedt, Mr. Leuthstrom, and I attended a Bible class. The Rev. Mr. Greenwald preached an excellent and edifying sermon.

December 25, Christmas Day. Service in church today was conducted by Dr. Reynolds. The service was preparatory to Holy Communion, which will be celebrated tomorrow, on Sunday. The Christmas message of Christ's birth brings a deep sense of joy and exaltation to the heart of the Christian believer. My thoughts today are with my loved ones in Sweden.

December 26, Sunday, Second Day of Christmas. Today we celebrated the Lord's Supper at our service. The Rev. Mr. Greenwald preached an exceptionally good sermon. What a wonderful comfort and assurance is ours in the Word of God and the holy sacraments which speak to us of the ever present Savior. May a gracious God help me to find my strength and succor in his means of grace.

December 31. This is the last day of the year 1852. It has

rained all day and has been cold and uncomfortable. During the past week I have diligently studied my Greek and other subjects for school. God has certainly been kind to me during the past year. I have received much new and useful knowledge, and though there have been some perplexities and problems, there has been far greater joy. Farewell to you, old year of 1852!

The Third Year at Columbus

The Year 1853
Time is fleeting, grasp the light
While the light is nigh;
Call upon the Lord of might,
In heaven he hears thy cry.

January 1. I begin this New Year in the name of Jesus. I thank thee, heavenly Father, for thy many blessings bestowed upon me in the days that are past. I humbly acknowledge my unworthiness of thy rich goodness. Thou hast promised all those who trust in thee that thou wilt be near them always, even unto the end of the world. Therefore with new courage I now continue my studies. Bless and keep me and my loved ones. In the name of Jesus. Amen.

January 5. On this day classes at school resumed after the holiday recess. A number of new students are enrolled for the spring semester. I am taking a course in mathematics this term.

January 7. I became very ill during the night with a severe headache and aches and pains in my entire body. I was sure that I was dying. If death is my lot, I know that I am a saved soul because my dear Savior has redeemed me and rescued me from sin, death, and the devil and has fulfilled every demand of the law in my stead. He has promised that all those who believe in him shall not perish but shall have everlasting life. My sins have been forgiven and I can die in peace. If I should die I want to say a loving farewell to my loved ones, Father, Mother, brothers, and sisters, and to all my friends and benefactors and wish for them God's richest blessings and eternal salvation in Christ.

January 8. My illness apparently was not unto death. I felt well enough to get out of bed this morning and go up to school. But after returning to my room again I felt weak and ill.

January 9. I arose early and attended public worship at church in the morning. Heard a sermon by Dr. Reynolds on the theme, "The law was given through Moses, but grace and truth came by Jesus Christ." The sermon was so long, however, that there was very little edification in it for anyone. The preacher spent too much time on historical details. If I ever become a preacher I shall be careful not to preach long sermons. When people begin to cough and clear their throats, look at their watches, and especially to yawn, it does more harm than good to continue preaching.

January 30. A beautiful Sunday. The past week has brought us unusually fine weather. My studies at school have progressed satisfactorily, and I have enjoyed very good health. The Rev. Mr. Greenwald delivered the sermon at divine service this forenoon on the necessity of becoming a member of the church. I did not approve of this sermon because it emphasized what man must do and accomplish, what our duty and responsibility must be, instead of stressing what we are and what we have in Jesus Christ. I realize that Greenwald did not mean that we can earn our own righteousness before God, but this is precisely the impression which such a sermon might well leave upon the hearts and minds of many hearers. This same emphasis I have heard altogether too often from our English Lutheran ministers, and it seems to prevail in general throughout our English churches.

February 20. On Monday of this week my friend and countryman, Mr. Rystedt, left town to go to Australia in search of gold. He has hopes of accumulating enough gold to go back to Sweden and settle down there. This may be a good idea, but I do not approve of his method of finding wealth. It is too much of a gamble. I was nevertheless loath to part from this friend, for he is a true and genuine Swede who holds to Swedish values and ideals. He possesses an excellent education and a sterling character. On Wednesday evening I attended a meeting on spiritualism. I am far from being convinced about the truth and validity of this form of religion. I shall study this matter further.

April 29. The convention of the Evangelical Lutheran Joint Synod of Ohio has been meeting in Columbus during the past week. I have attended the sessions as often as possible to see how the Lutheran church in America conducts its affairs. Most of the pastors and lay delegates are Germans, and the German language is used almost exclusively. Those who are unable to use German are permitted to speak English.

The business sessions have been concerned with the liturgy, the educational institution here in Columbus, and Christian missions. Much discussion was given to the question whether the Joint Synod should join the General Synod. The following resolution was finally adopted: "That, whereas the General Synod does not stand on firm Lutheran ground, no steps can be taken to affiliate with this organization. No delegates will hereafter be sent to the General Synod."[9] Although this resolution passed, it was opposed by the English-speaking pastors. The synod will assemble again in 1855.

May 7. This day will undoubtedly constitute an important milestone in my life. I have this day received a communication which in all likelihood will determine the direction my life will henceforth take. Hitherto it has been my intention to return after a few years to Sweden, to live and die in my fatherland. But I have now received a letter from my parents informing me of their plans to sell out and come to America. This means that I shall never again see my native land, never have the opportunity of living and work-

[9] On the Joint Synod and the General Synod, see below, p. 143, n. 1.

ing there as I had hoped. Can this be true? Can it be possible? What a melancholy thought! Must I now behold the eventual loss of a genuine and noble Swedish heritage as it becomes mingled with and eventually absorbed by an American tradition? Will it mean, as far as my family is concerned, that our Swedish inheritance will be lost, buried, and forgotten? God forbid! To be sure, my family will find here in America some advantages in both temporal and spiritual affairs, but I am certain that we and our descendants will undoubtedly become Americanized, and it is this that pains me. I have no quarrel with emigration from the old country except that those who come here soon lose their sense of identity with the homeland, forget the language of their forefathers, and no longer possess those unique qualities which characterize a genuine Scandinavian. As for myself, I shall struggle against this tendency, but who is strong enough to stand against the tide of the times? I shall write my family and tell them that, if possible, I will meet them in New York and accompany them inland.

June 20. On this day the Rev. A. Wiberg paid me a visit. He was formerly a true Lutheran minister but has now become a Baptist. Most regrettable! He arrived about two o'clock in the afternoon, and I received him cordially but not warmly. Since I had a class at 2:30 P.M. our conversation in these first few minutes was of a very general nature. He seemed to be avoiding any mention of religion. When I returned from class we resumed our visit and our conversation soon centered upon religion. He told me how he happened to become a Baptist. It seems that a tract by R. Pengilly entitled *Who Shall Be Baptized?* convinced him of Baptist views. He tried to set forth the basic principles of his Baptist faith, whereupon we began to argue about the doctrine of baptism without convincing each other of our respective views. It was clearly evident that he has given up entirely his former Lutheran faith. With respect to the Lord's Supper and the doctrine of election he is a

Calvinist, but he places the very greatest emphasis on the Baptist interpretation of the sacrament of baptism. He gave me three books, namely, Caron on *Baptism,* Hinton's *History of Baptism,* and Pengilly's *Who Shall Be Baptized?* For shame's sake I was compelled to thank him for this so-called gift. We were invited to have tea with Dr. Reynolds, and here Wiberg met not only Reynolds, but a number of others as well. Wiberg and Reynolds had a small argument about baptism, even as they discussed a number of other subjects. About eight o'clock in the evening I bade Wiberg farewell as he continued on his journey. My heart was filled with sadness as I thought about this man's apostasy from the faith of his fathers and the harm and confusion he would doubtless cause among many of my countrymen. What a blessing he could have been if he had remained faithful to the true faith. If bitter tears could help, I would be willing to shed them the rest of my life! Wiberg goes now to New York and thence back to Sweden, where he will spread his false and soul-destroying doctrines. May a merciful God spare his people from all error and establish them in his truth for the sake of Christ our Lord. Amen.

June 29. The past two days we have had examinations at school. We have come to the end of the term. It was announced that the fall term would begin on next September 14 and that we would assemble in the new building that is being built in Gooddale Park.

July 10. The past few weeks have been difficult and filled with anxiety. I must go to New York to meet my family, but have been unable to find any work to earn some money for my ticket and some decent clothes. I have had many conferences with Dr. Reynolds, the Rev. Mr. Spielmann, the Rev. Mr. Greenwald, and Professor Lehmann, but to no avail.

Finally Dr. Reynolds has loaned me twenty dollars and given me recommendations to several pastors in the East. The Rev. Mr. Spielmann also gave me a good recommendation to a book seller, Mr. Ludwig, in New York. I purchased a small satchel for one dollar and am now all packed and ready to leave Columbus for New York, where I hope to find some work while awaiting the arrival of my family.

It is now about three years since I arrived here in Columbus as a total stranger. I have studied diligently and have often done hard labor between school terms. Poverty has pressed me at every turn, and I have been compelled to live mostly on charity. But I have somehow managed to get along one day at a time. The future lies entirely in God's hand, and he alone knows if I will ever return here again. I hope I may do so, if it is God's will. Farewell, farewell, dear Capital University.

3

INTERIM OF WORK AND TRAVEL
1853-1854

July 12, 1853. This morning I paid a visit to Dr. Reynolds, the Rev. Emmanuel Greenwald, and the Rev. C. Spielmann and bade them goodbye. I then returned to my roominghouse and said farewell to Mrs. La Zalle, who was the only member of the family at home at that hour. I hurried to the depot, purchased a ticket to New York for $14.40, and at 10:40 A.M. I left Columbus with a light heart and high hopes for the future.

En route to Cleveland we passed through Delaware, Marion, Galion, and Shelby, small towns along the way. Our course took us through a sparsely cultivated countryside, much of which is covered with native timber. Cleveland, which undoubtedly will some day become a very great metropolis, is already a sizable lake port terminal, attractively situated on the shores of Lake Erie.

Arriving in Cleveland about 4:30 P.M., we continued on our way eastward, passing through Plainfield, Ashtabula, State Line, and Erie, Pennsylvania, arriving at Dunkirk, New York, during the night. At Dunkirk we caught the train for New York. The trip through the Allegheny Mountains was a glorious experience. The scenery was spectacular as our train wound its way through the steep precipices and deep valleys.

July 13. We arrived at Jersey City this afternoon. Here I

boarded the Hudson ferry bound for New York. I looked forward to seeing the great city once again. But when we reached New York harbor I was immediately surrounded by a noisy gang of young roughnecks who almost seemed to want to swallow me alive. They wanted to carry my valise, they wanted to direct me to a restaurant, they wanted to show me where I could find lodging, where I could get a job, etc. It is terribly dangerous for a green youngster like me, or anyone else for that matter, to fall into the clutches of such rascals whose only purpose is to swindle and defraud inexperienced travelers.

The only address which I had in New York was that of Professor H. I. Schmidt,[1] a friend of Dr. Reynolds, who lived on Twenty-second Street. After tearing myself away from my tormenters I caught a street car which took me in the direction I wanted to go. At the end of the car line I got off and walked a considerable distance before finally locating the right street and the right house. By this time I was not only tired and grimy after my long journey, but hungry and thirsty as well. Under such circumstances it was perhaps presumptuous and improper to knock at the door of such an elegant house, but I had no alternative. I stood on the front doorstep with fear and trembling, and presently the door was opened by the lady of the house. I noticed that she hesitated to let me in until she heard that I carried greetings to Dr. Schmidt from Dr. Reynolds. Dr. Schmidt was not at home at the moment, but I was invited to come in and wash and clean up a little.

After a while Dr. Schmidt returned home, but I found him to be a very quiet and reserved man who dressed well and made a fine appearance. Indeed, he was a professor at Columbia College in New York, and at the same time a Lutheran pastor widely

[1] Henry Immanuel Schmidt (1806-1889), a member of the New York Ministerium of the Lutheran church, was for many years professor at Columbia College, New York City.

known for his strict Lutheran confessionalism. He read my recommendations, talked briefly about sundry matters, but said absolutely nothing about the possibilities of my finding gainful employment in New York. He invited me to stay for dinner, and since I was extremely hungry, I accepted with profuse thanks. At the dinner table I ate somewhat sparingly and as politely and mannerly as I could.

After dinner I inquired about the address of the German bookseller, Heinrich Ludwig. It seemed to me that it was with a certain air of relief that he gave me Ludwig's address. He sent greetings to Ludwig and expressed the hope that I would find work there. I thanked these good people for their hospitality and took my leave, but I was beginning to feel that a poor, unknown student, with no money and no friends, would have no bed of roses in New York. With little difficulty I found Ludwig's bookstore and print shop at 45 Vesey Street.

I discovered that Henry Ludwig was a German-American, a man about forty-five years old with a congenial disposition and a quick temper. He was a staunch Lutheran and a member of a large German Lutheran congregation in New York. It was easy to talk to him; he told me quite frankly that it would doubtless be difficult to find a job in New York for the short time I intended to stay. I had been commissioned by the authorities at school in Columbus to solicit new subscribers for the newspaper *Lutheran Standard*.[2] Mr. Ludwig was of the opinion, however, that such a solicitation would be very difficult.

This kind man invited me to stay overnight in his home, located in the northern section of the city. I accepted with alacrity, but in the meantime I wanted to look around town and visit the harbor area to see if any immigrant ships from Sweden had arrived

---

[2] The *Lutheran Standard*, published under the direction and supervision of the Board of Directors of Capital University, had as its purposes to encourage education and "to defend and explain the doctrines of the Lutheran Church as exhibited in the Augsburg Confession."

in port, but there were none. Later in the day I returned to the bookstore and accompanied Mr. Ludwig to his home, where I was graciously received by Mrs. Ludwig and the children. Here I had good food and restful lodging. There are some Germans who are unusually hospitable and friendly.

July 14. Right after breakfast I set out to find the Rev. John Schock, pastor of the St. James English Lutheran church here in town. I wanted to ask him about the possibilities of securing subscriptions for the *Lutheran Standard* in his congregation. He received me with friendliness, and we had a long visit. He is about forty years old, unmarried, and makes his home with a widow, all members of whose family belong to his congregation. He is not a cold person, but rather sympathetic, even though he is not particularly talkative. He promised to recommend the *Standard* to his people and invited me to return for supper and to spend the night in his home. Thereupon, I went back down town to see if any immigrant ships had yet arrived, but found nothing. After spending the day seeking subscribers for the *Standard* and interviewing Mr. Ludwig about selling some books for him in Pennsylvania, I returned to the residence of the Rev. Mr. Schock, where I spent the night. The more I learned to know this man the more I liked him. Both he and his friends were kind and hospitable to me.

July 15. After breakfast I made my way to Mr. Ludwig's bookstore, where I found him overwhelmed with work, but he took time to select some good books, such as Luther's *Postils* in German,[3] a few devotional books, several prayer manuals, and a number of Lutheran publications in English. With this load to carry, I left the bookstore, took the ferry to Elizabeth, New Jersey, where I caught the train for Easton, Pennsylvania. Easton was to be my

[3] In order to provide both clergy and laity with sound, evangelical sermons, Martin Luther prepared collections of brief sermons which were widely distributed and read. These volumes were called *Postils*.

headquarters where I could leave my supply of books while canvassing the surrounding area as a book salesman.

As a book peddler I have encountered two serious obstacles. On the one hand there is the theological indifference of New Lutheranism. My books are genuinely Lutheran, and therefore do not please the liberal and rationalistic New Lutherans.[4] On the other hand there is the prevailing parsimony of the people who declare that they cannot afford to buy books. Indeed, I have met some folks, especially among the older German farmers, who would like to have Luther's *Postils,* but when I try to make a sale they will immediately say, "It costs too much." And how they can haggle. Very often I throw off my commission just to lighten the burden of books which I carry.

July 22. I have now completed the canvass of this community. Despite many obstacles I have succeeded in selling most of my books, and fortunately I have collected enough to cover my own expenses and to pay Mr. Ludwig what I owe him. I returned to Easton and took the early train today back to New York. After settling my account with Mr. Ludwig, I went down to the harbor to inquire if any immigrant ships had recently docked. There was an immigrant group which had just arrived from Gothenburg. This little flock was now ready to be shipped like cattle to the western regions of the country. They had contracted with an unreliable transportation company for the journey to Chicago at a cost of seven dollars per person. Poor people! They will doubtless have their share of trouble along the way.

Today I bargained with a Mr. William Johnson for board and room at a cost of two dollars a week for the time I am here in New York. This is as reasonable a rate as I can hope to find, but even then I will have nothing with which to pay if I can find no work here. May God help me.

[4] In the eyes of conservative Lutherans, "New Lutherans" were those who gave historic Lutheran doctrine a liberal, rationalistic interpretation.

July 27. Today I set out to look for the Rev. Anders Wiberg, and I finally found him at the home of a Baptist minister by the name of Steward who lives on Cherry Street. Wiberg seemed pleased to see me again, and when I told him about my predicament he promised to help me find employment in the city. He then handed me a book on baptism.

July 28. Today Wiberg and I set out together to look for work. He escorted me to a wealthy ship owner, a millionaire who has a large fleet of vessels plying the seas. His name is Smith, and he is a zealous Baptist who has given liberal support to Baptist missions at home and abroad. He lives in a palatial home, and since we arrived there in the evening just before meal time, we were invited to stay for supper. Wiberg was apparently a beloved and respected guest in the Smith home, and everyone made a big fuss over him, as if he were a rich prize they had won from the Swedish Lutherans.

Since I was in Wiberg's company, and a Swede at that, I was also included in the dinner invitation. So we dined in most elegant surroundings with our aristocratic hosts, and for the first, and undoubtedly the only, time in my life I ate with a gold knife, fork, and spoon. But because of my ragged and ill-fitting clothing I felt ill at ease and very much out of place. In the meantime, however, it was decided that I should go to work for Mr. Smith in his Wall Street establishment at a salary of two dollars a week, which would just cover my room and board. In my dire circumstances this was, to be sure, a real help, but I still needed new clothes. Nevertheless, I am deeply grateful to God who has not forgotten me in my extremity.

August 16. I have not made any entries in my diary for several weeks. I have been so busy the whole of every day that when evening comes I am too tired to write in my diary. I have now been at Mr. Smith's office on Wall Street for several weeks, from early morning until late evening. A great many interesting people pass through the office—merchants, bankers, ship captains, ship owners, ministers, professors, and many others from all corners of the world—and therefore one can learn a great deal by keeping eyes and ears open. My boss, Mr. Smith, is an object lesson to me. No wonder he is nervous and often distracted, living as he does in such a swirling turmoil of activity. He is a study in contradictions.

On the one hand he evidences an almost unlimited confidence in me. Here I am, a poor, ragged immigrant boy, running errands for my boss which sometimes involve carrying large sums of money and bags of gold to be deposited in the bank, to be paid to various creditors, or to buy drafts. Fortunately, I have never been robbed of a penny. I firmly believe that God has protected me, but my ragged, ill-fitting clothes have doubtless been of help too, since no one would suspect that such a bedraggled beggar-boy carries anything really valuable on his person. One evening Mr. Smith sent me out in the darkness to find a ship in the harbor which was just ready to sail for India. A group of Baptist missionaries was on board, and I was to bring them some drafts and other valuables before sailing time. I scurried through the dark streets and alleys, through gangs of dock workers and ruffians, before finding the right vessel. It was no easy task, and I did not return to my room until very late at night. But God has been with me to guide and protect.

Mr. Smith has indeed evidenced an unusual degree of confidence in me. But on the other hand he has never once uttered a single word of appreciation or thanks. From him I receive only two dollars a week. But if I make the slightest mistake, or misunderstand his orders, then he flies into a rage and overwhelms me with a veritable storm of abuse and vituperation. In such moments I am sure that only a dog should serve such a master, and if I had any other prospects for work I would certainly leave Mr. Smith's employ. But now I have no choice. I must swallow my medicine with silence and patience. In the very next moment after one of his fits of temper, Mr. Smith can turn completely around and again show me the most complete confidence. There is some comfort for me in the knowledge that Mr. Smith treats all of his employees in this same impulsive way.

Today I learned that a company of Swedish immigrants from the province of Småland has landed in New York. Their leader is said to be the Rev. Erland Carlsson,[5] and they have already left the city for the west. It seems likely that the Rev. Mr. Carlsson will settle in Chicago, for there are many Swedish settlers there who need the services of a faithful shepherd.

August 30. Today I quit my job at Smith's office. I must either find some remunerative employment or move away from here. Poverty is a trying burden. In old Sweden I knew nothing of real poverty, for though my parents were not wealthy, we always had enough to supply our needs. In contrast, here in America, and especially here in New York during this past summer, I have tasted real poverty. In such deprivation one needs to have an unusually sturdy faith in God if one is not to sink into despair and turn either to suicide or into paths of dishonesty. As for myself, I can never thank God enough for having so mercifully helped me in time of trouble and need. But dire poverty is often the reason for trying many foolish and imprudent schemes to make a little money. This was the motive for the stupid attempt I made some time ago in all seriousness to publish some poems and songs I had written in the hope that I could sell enough copies to get sufficient income to buy some decent clothes and a ticket to Chicago. I sought out the editor of a small paper, *Skandinavian,* whose name is Mr. A. G. Öbom, whose establishment is located at 92 Cliff Street. Öbom is a thin little man with a black beard who came to this country from the province of Dalsland, Sweden. He is married to a Swiss woman, and they have a very large family. The marks

---

[5] Erland Carlsson (1822-1893), pioneer Swedish pastor in Chicago, and one of the founders of the Augustana Lutheran Church.

of poverty are evident on every hand. The print shop is a very small, cluttered room where the entire family lives, cooks, eats, sleeps, and works. The little paper is published only occasionally, and as a newspaper it is a sorry looking sheet. Mr. Öbom, who is a shy and reticent man, promised to print my poems and songs for twenty dollars. I tried to borrow this amount from several people, but did not succeed, fortunately. It is downright amazing how foolish one can become in moments of panic.

For the past several days New York has sweltered in a heat wave. A number of people have died because of heat prostration. In this city one can see, on the one hand, the very greatest wealth and luxury, and on the other, the most terrible poverty. These large metropolitan centers contain, indeed, they consist of, sewers of sin, shame, and misery, and yet there are people who thrive here.

September 12. The time I have spent here in New York waiting for the ship that will bring my relatives to America has been exceedingly tedious and wearisome. Several ships have arrived from time to time, bringing large and small groups of immigrants, but there has been no word of my loved ones. During this time in the city I have seen many interesting sights, including the World's Fair at the Crystal Palace. I also went over to Brooklyn several times to see the city and especially to visit the beautiful cemetery, "Greenwood." I even visited the United States Navy Yard, which proved unusually interesting. On Sundays I have usually attended services at St. James English Lutheran church, where I have often heard the Rev. Mr. Schock preach. I have also attended services at the large German Lutheran church where the Rev. Dr. Stohlmann is the minister.[6] On a few occasions I have gone to the "Bethel Ship" for afternoon or evening services and heard the Rev. Olof

[6] K. F. E. Stohlmann (1810-1868) was pastor of St. Matthew's Lutheran Church in New York City from 1838 to 1868 and a prominent figure in the New York Ministerium.

Hedstrom or some visiting pastor bring the message. There is one thing, however, that I find regrettable about so many of the sermons I hear, and that is the way the distinction between law and gospel is obscured. This can result in nothing but religious confusion.

I have finally concluded that I can remain here in the city no longer. I must leave and be on my way. I have settled my account with my landlord, Mr. Johnson, and then borrowed $6.50 from the Rev. Mr. Schock for my ticket to Chicago.

From New York to Chicago

September 14. Leaving New York by the same route I had taken when I came out East three years ago, I headed for Buffalo, and according to my ticket I was to travel to Chicago via the Great Lakes. But I actually felt too weak to travel such a distance on the open deck, and I have no money with which to buy food during such an extended journey. The future has looked dark, indeed.

Upon reaching Buffalo, however, I found at least a partial solution to my problems. I looked up the well-known Lutheran pastor in Buffalo, the Rev. J. A. A. Grabau of the Buffalo Synod,[7] and told him about my predicament. He wrote a note for me to take to the office of the transport company, requesting them to send me to Chicago by the shorter route via Toledo. This request was granted, so I had now only to cross Lake Erie, but this was bad enough since I was compelled to spend the night on the open deck of the ship in a driving rainstorm. By this time I had gone without food for many hours. Tired and wet I lay down on a board which was somewhat sheltered from the wind and rain. I slept for

[7] J. A. A. Grabau (1804-1879), pioneer German Lutheran pastor in Buffalo, New York, and long-time professor at the "German Lutheran Martin Luther College" in Buffalo, was the founder and first president of the Buffalo Synod. Organized in 1845, the Buffalo Synod was originally composed largely of immigrants from Prussia who, as "Old Lutherans," were staunchly loyal to the Lutheran confessions.

several hours, but awakened during the night with a severe headache and chills.

September 15. A clear day. My headache is somewhat better. We arrived in Toledo about 4 P.M. A German traveling companion had noticed that I was hungry and had no food, so he offered me a piece of bread and a slice of sausage. It is wonderful how God can provide help for our needs.

Toledo is a relatively new city, situated on the northwest bank of the Maumee River, with a population of about five thousand. There are four churches, including a Roman Catholic, an Episcopal, a Methodist, and a Presbyterian congregation. Since my train did not leave until the next morning, I found lodging for the night in a rooming house operated by a respectable Irishman. During the night I became very ill, but the landlord gave me the best of care so that I was able to board the train in the morning.

September 16. We left Toledo at 8 A.M. I had neither food nor money, and there was no telling how long it will take the slow and pokey immigrant train to reach Chicago. Our course has taken us through the northwest corner of Ohio where the terrain seems to be covered with dense forest. About noon we entered the state of Michigan, and now we passed along marshes, swamps, and then on into rolling hills. One of my traveling companions was a very talkative and friendly Welshman, who had a well-filled lunch basket which he insisted that I share with him, since there was enough, he said, for both of us. Here was a further evidence of God's merciful providence, and my heart was filled with gratitude.

September 17. About 8 P.M. we entered the State of Indiana. Here the topography is different from what we have seen in Ohio and Michigan. There are broad, level, and undoubtedly fertile plains. La Porte was the first city we entered in Indiana. In time this place will doubtless be an important metropolis. Before long we crossed over into Illinois. The scenery was spectacularly beautiful as we rounded the southern tip of Lake Michigan and approached the city of Chicago. At 2 P.M. we were entering this remarkable metropolis. After an absence of three years I have come again to this place. What is it that makes this city so attractive to me? There are no towering buildings, such as in New York. On the contrary, Chicago consists of an innumerable cluster of ordinary wooden buildings spread out over an immense level plain. And it is growing, growing, growing, so rapidly that it is almost unbelievable. If this expansion continues, Chicago will surely become in the next fifty years the world's largest city.

After bidding farewell to my kind fellow-traveler, the Welshman, whose name was Jones, I set off for the north section of the city in search of the Rev. Erland Carlsson, of whom I had heard much, but whom I had never met. I finally met a Swede on the street who was able to direct me to Carlsson's residence. I found the pastor living in the home of a fine Norwegian family on Des Plaines Street. Carlsson received me with the very greatest kindness and showed me so much love and sympathy that I was actually surprised. Here I was met not only with gracious words, but with deeds of love. He insisted that I should make my home with him. I told him how penniless and poverty-stricken I was, and that I had nothing wherewith to pay for my keep. Indeed, I said that I had nothing but the rags on my back and my Greek New Testament, which I took out of my pocket and showed him. With tears in his eyes he said to me, "You are most heartily welcome to stay here with me." This heart-warming love and kindness was a balm to my poor, sick heart and spirit, for my poverty had been so desperate that I had nearly been driven to despair. My meeting with the Rev. Mr. Carlsson occurred on Saturday, September 17, and I shall never forget that hour.

September 18. On this Sunday I have had the opportunity of hearing Carlsson preach two times; in the forenoon he delivered a sermon in the Norwegian Lutheran church on Superior Street, and in the afternoon he preached to the Swedish congregation which met in the same building. What a wonderful experience for me to share again in a Swedish Lutheran service and to listen once more to an excellent doctrinal sermon in my mother tongue after being deprived of this privilege for three years. Indeed, it was really out of this world! That God has sent a man like Carlsson to Chicago at a time like this seems to me to be a miracle of divine providence. The spiritual deprivation among our countrymen here is very great, but this servant of God possesses just those qualifications which the work here seems to require. I can easily imagine the great accomplishments this man is destined to fulfill here. May the Lord grant him humility and sufficient strength for his tasks.

We have discussed the desirability of establishing a Swedish parochial school here, and we have agreed that I am to conduct such a school during the fall term while I await the arrival of my relatives. Carlsson is quick about making decisions and therefore announced today that a meeting will be held tomorrow evening in the Norwegian church for the purpose of taking action regarding the school.

September 19. The Rev. Mr. Carlsson and I have thus far had opportunity to discuss only briefly our experiences here in America, the prevailing conditions in Sweden, and the prospects for our work in the city. Carlsson, who has been here only about a month, is eager to learn what I know about the Swedes in America and about the Lutheran church in this country.

This evening we held the school meeting in the Norwegian church. The business at hand was quickly disposed of. It was decided that we should start a parochial school to instruct children in Swedish or Norwegian language studies, and also to offer courses in religion, particularly Bible history, catechism, etc. A suitable building is to be secured and I was elected to be the teacher. The salary will doubtless be somewhat uncertain since each child will be charged a certain fee, and the income will depend, therefore, on the number that are enrolled.

October 1. Sunday. My health has been somewhat precarious, and I have suffered from fever and chills. Carlsson is absent from the parish and therefore, as his substitute, I have been preaching at the evening services. This is the first preaching I have done in Chicago. I am afraid I have not done too well.

I have now been teaching school for one week. What a motley crowd of students. Some of the children are Norwegian, and they naturally use their mother tongue. Some are Swedish and use their own language. Still others are neither Norwegian nor Swedish and must use only the English language. On the whole they are an undisciplined lot, and some of them are real hellions. To succeed with these youngsters requires much patience, wisdom, and love.

November 8. A few days ago I received a letter from my relatives informing me that they had landed in New York and were on their way to Chicago. This evening I received word that they were now here in the city. I hurried to the depot and found them at a German rooming house nearby. This reunion with my dear family on American soil was an indescribable experience. It was a moment of unspeakable joy for me, but at the same time a moment of immeasureable anguish in the realization that we were now homeless strangers in a foreign land, and that we were now bereft of our dear, peaceful, old home in Norrbäck.

November 17. For the past several days I have had my hands full worrying about my family and running around town trying to find lodging for my relatives. We have decided that it might be best, for the time being, for them to stay in Chicago during this winter. Some of them have found jobs and seem to be getting along fairly well.

November 29. This morning I attended a religious service and heard Elling Eielsen himself preach in the Norwegian chapel.[8] He is a big, tall, strong man in the prime of life, and seems to have strength enough for almost anything. I noticed that as he strode across the prairie to the chapel his friend and assistant, Rasmussen, walked behind him, stepping exactly in his tracks. This was an indication of respectful discipleship. I felt that the service was inordinately long. First a hymn of fourteen verses was sung very slowly. Then a portion of Scripture was read, followed by a long prayer. Thereupon another long hymn. Then Elling read a long sermon from a book by H. N. Hauge,[9] and followed this with a long sermon of his own. At this point another hymn was sung. Thereafter assistant Rasmussen stepped forward and delivered a fervent, emotional address, after which the service was concluded with prayer, the benediction, and another hymn. It was indeed a very long service, and I marveled at the congregation's forbearance. There was no evidence of restlessness or impatience, and most of the people sat perfectly still and stared at the floor at their feet. Elling's sermon was earnest and forthright, but he confused law and gospel as so many of the older pietists have been accustomed to do.

December 20. My brother, Andrew, came from Moline this day. He suggested that it would be advisable for our relatives to return with him to Moline rather than remain in Chicago over the winter. After a great deal of discussion it was so decided and accordingly they all departed for Moline. As for me, I have continued to teach school, living in the schoolroom on Kinzie Street and preparing my own meals. My board has consisted chiefly of tea and

[8] Elling Eielsen (1804-1883), a Lutheran evangelist who came to America from Norway in 1839. The Lutheran synod which he founded in 1846 was known as the "Eielsen Synod."

[9] Hans Nielsen Hauge (1771-1824), lay evangelist and leader of the evangelical revivals which swept through Norway during the early decades of the nineteenth century. See Joseph M. Shaw, *Pulpit Under the Sky* (Minneapolis: Augsburg, 1955).

crackers, and when I have wanted to add to my diet I have treated myself to a pint of syrup.

The Memorable Year of 1854

January 1, 1854. The New Year begins with very cold weather. No Swedish services have been held in the Lutheran church because the Rev. Mr. Carlsson is in St. Charles and Geneva, Illinois, during the New Year holiday conducting services in the newly organized congregation in that community.

At this time I have decided to stay on for the time being in Chicago in order to continue with my school teaching. I now am offering courses in English to older students. Half a score have enrolled, among whom is Per Holm, a surveyor from the Swedish province of Jämtland, Håkan Svedberg from Blekinge, C. G. Värnström from Småland, John Nilsson, and others. They are diligent and well-behaved students. From early morning until 5 P.M. in the evening we study Goodrich's *Third Reader*, a summary of the history and geography of the United States. We read and translate every word, over and over again, carefully memorizing every detail. Whether this is a good method or not may be open to question, but I shall be satisfied if at the end of the term most of these students can read and understand the English language quite well. They will then have received what they desired from this course of study.

January 4. This evening the Rev. T. N. Hasselquist, the Rev. L. P. Esbjörn, and several Norwegian ministers assembled here in Chicago for a conference. I think this is the second time the representatives of the Swedish and Norwegian congregations in Illinois have met together since they affiliated with the Synod of Northern Illinois.[10] Hasselquist preached the evening sermon. This

[10] The Synod of Northern Illinois was organized in Cedarville, Stephenson County, Illinois, September 18, 1851. It was divided into three conferences, each of which represented a national group. The Rock River Conference in-

is the first time I have seen and heard this man. He has a stately bearing and is an excellent speaker and preacher. Since I had not seen Esbjörn for three years it was also a very pleasant privilege to meet him again. He hasn't changed much, except that he is perhaps an even more strict Lutheran than ever before.

January 5. The conference convened this day and will continue in session until next Monday evening. I had the honor of being received as a member of the delegation and was permitted to participate in the deliberations. The minutes of this conference will be published and distributed to our people. Esbjörn has been very insistent that I shall come to Andover as soon as I have concluded the school term.[11]

March 1. How time flies! My students have requested me to continue the school term for an additional two weeks, for which they are willing to pay me fifteen dollars. I have accepted this proposition and will keep on with the school another two weeks.

March 20. Today I left Chicago accompanied by my friend and fellow-countryman, Peter Holm. We went to Geneseo via the Chicago-Rock Island Railroad, the only line between Chicago and Rock Island. The fare was $4.75. At Geneseo we hired a livery rig to take us to Andover, at a cost of five dollars. After an absence of three years it was indeed a pleasure to see our many Andover friends and to visit in the home of the Rev. Mr. Esbjörn.

cluded the German and American pastors and their congregations, the Chicago Conference was composed of the Norwegians, and the Mississippi Conference included the Swedish pastors and their congregations. The Chicago and Mississippi conferences frequently held joint sessions and came to be known as "The United Scandinavian Conference." The conference meeting to which Norelius here refers was held in the Norwegian Lutheran church in Chicago, January 4-9, 1854. The minutes of this joint session constitute the earliest extant record of the United Scandinavian Conference. For an English translation of these minutes see *Augustana Historical Society Publications*, Vol. X, pp. 89 ff. It was the two Scandinavian conferences which in 1860 merged to form the Lutheran Augustana Synod.

[11] At this meeting of the United Scandinavian Conference the name of Eric Norelius is inscribed on the official roster of the Mississippi Conference, marking his identification with the Swedish community in America which was destined to form the Augustana Synod.

Some important changes have taken place since I was last here. The population has markedly increased; large tracts of land have been brought under cultivation; a brick church has been built, and the congregation has flourished.

March 27. Old man Jon Anderson drove me to Moline this day. In Moline I have many friends and acquaintances. Unfortunately a number of them have become Baptists and are eager to argue with me.

March 30. While here in Moline I have preached several times in the little Swedish Lutheran church and have even baptized a child. After C. J. Valentine, who was licensed by the Synod of Northern Illinois, moved from Moline to Princeton some time ago, the congregation here has had no resident pastor. Esbjörn tries to visit this parish as often as possible. This is the reason I have been invited to preach here and to administer baptism when necessary.[12]

April 28. Today I conducted catechetical examinations in the eastern section of the Andover parish and preached in the Andover church on Saturday evening, April 27. During these days we have received new reports from Iowa and Minnesota. One communication came from the Swedish people in St. Paul, Minnesota, reporting that a Swedish Lutheran congregation had been formed there, and asking for advice and help in securing a minister. It was stated that the number of Swedish settlers in Minnesota totals about six hundred. This letter, which was signed by Frank Mobeck, C. J. Lindstrom, P. M. Anderson, and A. J. Ekman, I was asked to translate into English in order that it might be published in the *Lutheran Standard*.

May 1. My friend Peter Holm and I went to Bishop Hill today

---

[12] This was an emergency arrangement since Norelius was not yet licensed to function as a clergyman. He did not receive such a license until the Chicago-Mississippi Conference meeting in Chicago, April 12-15, 1855. Cf. *ibid.*, p. 103.

to see how the Erik Jansonites[13] are faring. We arrived at the colony dormitory about noon. The colony consists of about seven hundred people who own and control some ten sections of land, some seventy horses, and about six hundred head of cattle. There is also a mill powered by a twenty-five horsepower steam engine which can grind about five hundred bushels of grain a day. The colony also operates a broom factory, a carpenter shop, a good blacksmith shop, a small tannery, and a spinning and weaving mill. The community consists of several brick residences and a large communal dormitory with many cell-like sleeping rooms. There is also a large dining hall in the basement of the communal dormitory where we saw about five hundred people eating. They were being served huge bowls of vegetables and platters piled high with pork.

Our guide was a former factory inspector from Forsa, in the province of Helsingland, Sweden. His name is J. E. Lundquist. He was very frank, speaking freely and with some emotion about the sufferings of the Jansonites, their persecution in Sweden, and their struggles in America. As a pious Jansonite he bemoaned the fact that the good, old piety of an earlier day was gradually giving way to a more secular spirit and to worldly ambition which seeks only the achievement of economic prosperity.

The Jansonite church is a wooden structure, since it is contrary to Jansonite doctrine to worship God in stone structures. The chapel is situated on the third story of the building and is fur-

---

[13] In 1846 Eric Janson or Jansson (1808-1850), eccentric lay leader of a separatistic movement in Sweden, founded a communal colony on a tract of land in Illinois which was given the name of Bishop Hill, after the name of Janson's birthplace in Sweden. On May 13, 1850, Janson was shot to death in the county courthouse at Cambridge, Illinois, by a disgruntled former follower. The colony continued as a communal endeavor until its dissolution in 1879. For another firsthand account of the colony see *Pioneering Adventures of Johan Edvard Lilljeholm in America 1846-1850*, trans. Arthur Wald (Rock Island, Ill.: Augustana Historical Society, 1962), pp. 13-19, 29-34. See also Michael A. Mikkelsen, *The Bishop Hill Colony: A Religious Communistic Settlement in Henry County, Illinois* (Baltimore: Johns Hopkins Press, 1892).

nished with a pulpit, chancel, and balcony, where there is also a small reed organ. While we were in the chapel we discussed church order and polity, and old man Lundquist informed us that there are about twenty people in the colony who can preach, although there are three in particular who generally assume this responsibility. "Since the death of Janson," said he, "we no longer have a ruler or a patriarch but are more like a community of brethren." He also mentioned that the colony is planning a revision of their hymnbook because there are some grammatical and technical errors in the present edition.

Pointing to their land and goods the colonists claim to have a very good life, but most of the laborers, and especially the women, give the impression of being a listless and enslaved people. In contrast, however, a few of the men seem to be having a good time with plenty of leisure on their hands. The entire situation left me with a melancholy and depressed feeling, and I do not believe that the Bishop Hill colony faces a very bright future. I must say, however, that the colony people were most hospitable toward us and invited us to remain with them overnight, but we preferred to walk back to Andover, where we arrived late in the evening, tired and soaking wet from the rain which fell as we trudged our way home.

May 9. On this day I left Andover, having heard that the Rev. Erland Carlsson was planning on making a trip to Minnesota. Since he was coming by way of Moline and Rock Island, I hoped to meet him and accompany him on this journey. Although Carlsson had left before I arrived in Rock Island-Moline, several of my relatives decided to go with me to the Minnesota settlement of Chisago Lake.

May 15. We have waited for five days for a boat bound for Minnesota. On this day, however, a boat finally came, and for forty dollars we bought deck space to Stillwater, Minnesota, for ten people, one cow, and our luggage. We had not proceeded very far, however, before our river boat ran onto a sand bar, and we were stuck. We finally freed the vessel and proceeded upstream, but our boat is so heavily loaded that our progress is very slow. The countryside along the Mississippi River is beautiful.

May 21. This is Sunday. We have landed in St. Paul, Minnesota, having spent six days on the Mississippi since leaving Moline. St. Paul, a lively little city of about six thousand inhabitants, is situated high and dry on a sandstone cliff overlooking the Mississippi River. I have learned that the Rev. Erland Carlsson has already been here and is expected to return soon from Chisago Lake. He will then help the people to make arrangements for their religious affairs. I have been requested to conduct services, so this evening we assembled in an antiquated little schoolhouse on Jackson Street. There were quite a few people present and they seemed happy and hopeful.

May 22, Monday. We boarded a boat for Stillwater on this day, arriving at our destination late in the evening. We met several Norwegians but no Swedes. The lumberjacks, whose work in the woods is now finished, are everywhere present, and we see their bright red wool shirts at every turn. A young man wearing a bright red wool shirt with an embroidered front, a wide leather belt, and a plug hat is right in style here in the St. Croix Valley.

May 23. I rode the mail stage to the little village of Taylors Falls, and from there walked nine miles to Chisago Lake. Here at long last I have now beheld in this little three-year-old settlement the actual goal of the plans which I and my friends made back in old Sweden. To be sure, not much of a colony has yet developed here, but the natural location, with its beautiful lakes and pleasant climate, is attractive and inviting. On his recent visit to this community the Rev. Mr. Carlsson organized a Swedish Lutheran congregation, the first such in this part of the State of Minnesota. At the request of the people here, I have agreed to preach to the congregation on Sundays and conduct a parochial school during the week for the time being. We are to meet in the hayloft of Peter Berg's barn.

May 25. This is Ascension Day in the church year. I preached this day for the first time in Chisago Lake. In the afternoon I walked to Taylors Falls and conducted service there, returning to Chisago Lake this evening. The road through the forest is very poor, and the mosquitoes are so terrible that one can stand the trip only by covering head and face with a net of fine mesh.

June 4. When I arrived at Berg's hayloft for services this day I was met by a stately looking, venerable, gray-haired old man who introduced himself as "Agrelius, pastor from Sweden, now in the service of the Methodist church." It would undoubtedly have been polite for me to invite him to preach in my stead. But I could not do so because of my own personal convictions and also because the congregation has not granted me that prerogative. Therefore, I preached as usual, but no sooner had I concluded my sermon than Agrelius arose and delivered another sermon. Since I did not wish to create a disturbance, there was nothing to do but listen with as much patience as possible. And patience was certainly required to endure the drivel which he presented. With all due respect to the gray hair of Agrelius, I must say that his talk was unworthy of serious consideration. The substance of it was to point out how fortunate those Swedes are who have come to America. Here they are free to worship God according to conscience. In Sweden, however, there is always the imminent danger of the Russian bear. Russia and Sweden share a common border north of the Baltic Sea, and some fine day, declared Agrelius, the Russian bear will likely cross that border and give Sweden a fateful bear hug. Woe betide the Swedes living there then! The old man's political ruminations regarding the Russian bear were perhaps not too far fetched, but this kind of talk makes mighty thin spiritual fare. I have been told that Agrelius has offered the people a broad kind of ministry, saying, "If you prefer the Methodist way, I can give you that; but if you would rather have the Lutheran way, I can also give you that, because I have been a minister in Sweden for twenty-six years." As to his character, I have heard nothing derogatory.

June 17. On this Sunday just as I concluded the morning service a stranger arose in the audience and announced that he would conduct a religious service this afternoon. He had not consulted me or anyone else before making this announcement. This man was Fredrik O. Nilson, known as the first man to proclaim publicly in Sweden the doctrines of the Baptist church.[14] He had come to Minnesota and to Chisago Lake to win converts for the Baptist cause. His boorish manner of intruding upon us to announce his meeting, however, did not commend him to the community. Furthermore, he was not a gifted speaker, even though he was able to communicate his thoughts clearly and coherently.

September 10. This was my last Sunday in Chisago Lake. I preached on the text Revelation 3:14-22 and bade the congregation a heartfelt farewell. As a gratuity for my services I received twenty-five dollars from the people. I am returning to Moline and Rock Island in Illinois.

September 18. Today I arrived in Moline and arranged to stay here for a few weeks. There has been much sickness in Moline and Rock Island during this past summer. Cholera, malaria, and other diseases have been prevalent among the immigrants, and many have died.

The Baptists have been zealously at work among the Swedish people of this community in recent months. The little Lutheran congregaion which has no resident pastor has been very hard pressed. The methods which some of these fanatics have used in their endeavor to destroy the Lutheran congregation here are almost beyond description.

[14] Fredrik O. Nilson (1809-1881), pioneer Swedish Baptist lay evangelist, organized several Baptist congregations in Sweden and America.

September 26. This day I returned to Andover. I found the Rev. Mr. Esbjörn and his family in poor health. During the past months the weather has been very hot and there has been much sickness. A great many immigrants have arrived here, and not a few have been carried off by the cholera epidemic. Esbjörn's home and the undercroft of the church have been filled, week after week, with sick and dying newcomers. Discouragement and sadness seem to be engraved on every face.

October 1, Sixteenth Sunday after Trinity. I preached at Andover today on a most appropriate text for the many sorrowing people, namely, the comforting words of Jesus, "Woman, weep not." It was also my great privilege to receive the Lord's Supper, which I had missed all summer. The dear congregation, though poverty stricken, gave me an offering amounting to eleven dollars. I was indescribably encouraged by this act of benevolence.

October 2. This day I left Andover, accompanied by Esbjörn's youngest son Joseph. We are bound for Columbus to enroll in the school there. We arrived in Chicago toward evening. Here, as elsewhere, the dreaded cholera has raged and has not yet subsided. The streets are almost quiet and deserted, while the people we have seen look more like ghosts than human beings. I went directly to the cobbler, C. J. Anderson, on Kinzie Street in the hope of finding the Rev. Mr. Carlsson there, but I was informed that he has suffered a severe attack of cholera and has therefore moved to Geneva for the time being. I called on a number of my friends in Chicago and on every hand heard the same reports of sickness, death, and bereavement.

October 3. I went to Geneva to visit the Rev. Mr. Carlsson this day. I found him convalescing but still very weak and feeble. But in his spirit he was full of courage and joy. During the past summer many Swedish immigrants have settled in Geneva and the neighboring community of St. Charles. In general these are sturdy, responsible people. They do not yet have a church but are planning on building one as soon as possible.

October 6. I returned to Chicago yesterday. This evening I conducted services in the church here. Mr. A. Andreen, who is acting as Carlsson's assistant, informed me that during the past summer he and Carlsson visited some Swedish settlements in the vicinity of Lafayette, Indiana. He suggested that I stop off there for a visit on my way to Columbus, since my route east takes us through that city.

October 8. On this Sunday I conducted services at West Point, about ten miles from Lafayette, Indiana. We hired an old Methodist church for the service, and I was surprised to see so many Swedish families gathered for both the morning and the afternoon services. Many of those present seemed to be genuine Christians, and everyone seemed eager and anxious to hear the Word of God. The oldest settlers have been in the area about two years, but the majority have come within the past year. Very few have as yet purchased their own land. Most of them live in and around West Point, Attica, Montmorency, Lafayette, and Yorktown, all within a radius of about thirty miles. But even this distance is not too great to prevent them from attending services when they have the opportunity.

The Methodists, especially a man called "Father Nyman," have been busy in this section and have succeeded in enrolling a number of Swedish families as probationers for six months, but these people do not seem to be inclined to become Methodists.

October 10. On this day I returned to Capital University, Columbus, Ohio, just after a revolution had occurred in the school. The president, Dr. Reynolds, together with several professors who sided with him, have left the institution. The Rev. Mr. Spielmann and Professor Lehmann are now at the helm of the school and are in charge of the affairs of the Lutheran Joint Synod. The cause of the upheaval seems to have been both personal and political. Dr.

Reynolds, despite his considerable learning, is a vain, despotic, and irritable individual, unfit to be the head of an institution. He was unable to enforce the strict discipline which he sought to establish, and as a consequence has been the object of a good deal of ridicule and scorn.

The political contention involved the question of affiliation with the General Synod. Dr. Reynolds has been scheming in every possible way to get the Joint Synod of Ohio united with the General Synod. Though he has succeeded in creating factions on both sides of the question, he has been thwarted in his unionistic attempts by more prudent men in the Joint Synod.

During the previous term at school I took some theological subjects along with my college courses. Beginning now with the winter term, however, I am devoting my time entirely to theological studies. In the interim of my absence, Capital University has been moved to its new location in Gooddale Park, in the north section of the city. Here our quarters are adequate and comfortable. The library has been enlarged and is housed in an excellent room. This will prove to be a gold mine for me, because I have no money to purchase my own books.

4

MINISTER TO IMMIGRANTS
1855-1856

The Ministerial License

April 15, 1855. The Swedish Lutheran pastors in Illinois have decided to hold a united conference by meeting with the Norwegian brethren of the Synod of Northern Illinois. The meeting will take place in Chicago during the Easter season. I have also received an urgent invitation to attend this conference, and because of the great scarcity of ministers, I have been advised to apply to the Synod of Northern Illinois for a ministerial license, and thus officially enter the ministerium. L. P. Esbjörn, M. F. Hokanson, T. N. Hasselquist, Erland Carlsson, and, most recently, P. A. Cedarstam have all joined the Synod of Northern Illinois. What hinders me from following their example? Well, I have been opposed from the very beginning to union with the Synod of Northern Illinois, which is a branch of the General Synod, because of its equivocal acceptance of the Augsburg Confession as being only "mainly correct." My opposition to the General Synod has gradually increased during my stay in Columbus, where I have been associated with the Joint Synod of Ohio. Here the official confessional position is unequivocal and in harmony with those convictions which I have held since childhood and which were inculcated by evangelical Christians in my homeland.[1]

I have therefore earnestly considered joining the Joint Synod of Ohio when I would be ready to enter the ministry. I have mentioned these sentiments to Esbjörn, who in a letter dated March 6, 1855, responded, ". . . the foremost reason for your joining the Ohio Synod would be your own welfare. But, my dear brother, we must consider not only our own good, but that of others as well. . . . The truth is invincible, not when it speaks from afar, but when it directly confronts error. Thus, Jesus did not isolate himself only among his friends and disciples, but mingled with publicans and sinners. . . ."

Although this line of reasoning has not fully persuaded me, I have nevertheless consented to attend the Chicago Conference, to submit to examination, and to be licensed and admitted into the Synod of Northern Illinois. I do this in order to avoid a schism among our Swedish Lutheran forces, but with the firm intention of laboring meanwhile for the separation of our Scandinavian people from the Synod of Northern Illinois.

Besides me there are three other candidates who are presenting themselves for examination and licensing, namely, A. Andreen, A. G. Zethraeus, and a Norwegian brother, O. Anfinson. The examination was as thorough as circumstances permitted, and lasted for three days. As a part of the examination each candidate was required to deliver a brief sermon. It happened that the presenta-

[1] Norelius' objections to the synod of Northern Illinois and to its parent body, the General Synod, derived from his opposition to the equivocal position these bodies took toward the Lutheran confessions. In contrast to conservative Lutherans like Norelius, the General Synod and the Synod of Northern Illinois tended at this time to sympathize with the "American Lutheranism" of S. S. Schmucker which sought to modify the confessional position of the Lutheran Church in America so as to bring it into closer conformity with the broad tenets of the general Protestantism of that day. See S. S. Schmucker, *Fraternal Appeal to the American Churches*, ed. and with an introduction by Frederick K. Wentz (Philadelphia: Fortress, 1965).

tion by A. G. Zethraeus was a complete fiasco. The next day he admitted before the entire conference that he had neither knowledge nor personal experience concerning spiritual life, and he therefore withdrew his application, acknowledging that he was unsuited for the ministry. With respect to the other candidates, the conference decided that we should immediately be recommended to the president of the Synod, the Rev. Simon W. Harkey,[2] who was present at the meeting, for an ad interim license until the synodical meeting next fall. The license presented to me reads as follows:

LICENSURE

In nomine Jesu, Amen.

This certifies that Eric Norelius, after proper examination in theology and associated sciences by the Mississippi and Chicago Conferences of the Evangelical Lutheran Synod of Northern Illinois, has been recommended to me by said Conferences for licensure, and he is therefore and hereby authorized and licensed to preach the gospel of Jesus Christ and administer the holy sacraments according to the forms of the Evangelical Lutheran Church, until the next meeting of the Evangelical Lutheran Synod of Northern Illinois, wherever Jesus Christ, the great head of the church, may call him to labor.

Chicago, April 15, 1855
SIMON W. HARKEY,
President of said synod

From the minutes of the conference the following excerpt is taken: "At 4 P.M. the conference met to decide at which places the licensed candidates shall be stationed, partly because of the requests of the people themselves and partly for the purpose of commending them to the people's trust and good will. Ole Anfinson had been called by some Norwegians in Lisbon, Illinois, who intend to move from that place to Iowa in the neighborhood of Fort Des Moines. A. Andreen had a call from the Swedish Lutheran

[2] Simon W. Harkey (1811-1889) was a prominent Lutheran pastor, editor, and educator, a member of the faculty of Illinois State University at Springfield, and for a number of years president of the Synod of Northern Illinois.

congregations in Chicago, as Pastor Erland Carlsson's assistant. Eric Norelius was advised to go to Lafayette, Indiana. P. A. Cedarstam was advised to go to Minnesota."[3]

April 16. After the meeting in Chicago I went at once to Indiana, to the field which had been assigned to me by the conference, and I have been received with great joy and satisfaction by my dear countrymen in the five different communities which comprise the parish organized here by the Rev. Erland Carlsson on February 18, 1855. I have written a letter to the president of Capital University, the Rev. C. Spielmann, informing him of the step I have taken.

The Move to Minnesota

My term of service in my first parish has lasted for only one year, which, unfortunately, is all too often the case with young pastors. What is the reason for this? Among several possible reasons, one is particularly common. The pastoral life is envisaged as an ideal and beautiful career, which turns out, however, to be more theory than reality when put to the test in actual experience. Often the very opposite comes to pass. Then dejection and discouragement fill the heart, and nothing is apparent except mistakes and miscalculations. It is then that the young pastor wants to move, hoping that it will be better in another parish. And perhaps it actually does turn out better, for he has doubtless learned some valuable lessons in his first charge. For my part, I have had, in general, a good congregation, and have enjoyed the confidence of the people. The members are mostly poor settlers, widely scattered, the majority of them without permanent homes and unable to provide much of a salary for their pastor. But I am not concerned about a big salary. I know that conditions will be even more difficult in the field where I want to go. I can see

[3] English translation in *Augustana Historical Society Publications,* Vol. X, p. 105.

no bright prospects for the settlements in Indiana, and with this in mind I have encouraged the people to move away. Furthermore, I have had a peculiar and very strong desire to go and labor in the wilderness country of Minnesota.

On the last day of April, 1856, my wife and I left West Point, and I preached my farewell sermon in Lafayette on Ascension Day.[4] On May 2 we arrived in Chicago, where we stayed with Pastor Carlsson, who was living in his new home on Superior Street, which seemed like a real palace to us. We spent several pleasant and happy days here with our friends. On May 4 Brother A. Andreen came from Rockford. Sunday, May 6, was a festive day in the Lord's house, including the confirmation of the youths' class of catechumens. During the week vesper services were held every evening. On Monday evening the Rev. T. N. Hasselquist also arrived and took part in the festivities.

At this time it was agreed that the Synod of [Northern] Illinois was to assemble in Geneva, Illinois, for a special convocation for the purpose of considering the question of a Swedish professorship for the school at Springfield, Illinois. Accordingly, on May 7 we went to Geneva, Illinois, and there we met the Rev. L. P. Esbjörn, the Rev. O. J. Hatlestad, the Rev. Paul Andersen, the Rev. B. G. Bergenlund, Dr. Simon Harkey, the Rev. C. B. Theummel, and other members of the clergy of the Synod of Northern Illinois. The lay delegates were Mr. T. Stenholm, Mr. S. Frid, Mr. M. Munter, and Mrs. L. H. Norem.

The main concern of the meeting was the decision regarding the character of the proposed professorship. There was disagreement about this matter. On the one hand, the Scandinavians uncompromisingly required that the professor-elect must pledge to teach in conformity with the Word of God and the Augsburg Con-

---

[4] On June 10, 1855, Eric Norelius was united in marriage to Inga Lotta, the daughter of Peter Peterson of West Point, Indiana. At the time of their marriage Eric was twenty-one years old and Inga Lotta was seventeen. Their marriage lasted more than sixty years.

fession. The Americans, on the other hand, thought that this was too strict.[5] They did not wish to be bound by the Augsburg Confession and feared that such a decision would incur the displeasure of the General Synod and that as a consequence they might forfeit the General Synod's home mission support. They sought to wash their hands of the matter, however, by formulating a resolution in such a way as to give the impression that a compromise had been made simply to appease the Scandinavians, and that the Scandinavians would therefore have to bear the blame for such ill-advised action.

The meeting closed on Saturday, May 12. The next day, Pentecost Sunday, May 13, the church in Geneva was to be dedicated. Therefore Harkey, Hasselquist, Carlsson, Bergenlund, and I stayed on for the festivities. The others returned to their homes. Esbjörn went to Princeton in order to assist in settling a disturbance there which the Methodists had stirred up and which had been aggravated by a recent visit of the Rev. Olof G. Hedstrom from New York.

The service in Geneva was well attended, the weather was pleasant, and the occasion was most festive. The service began with a preparatory sermon by Bergenlund. He kept on so long, however, that Carlsson gave him a broad hint to say Amen by opening the Service Book to the Confession of Sins and laying the opened book before him on the altar rail. This had very little effect. Hasselquist gave the dedicatory sermon and, assisted by the other pastors, conducted the rite of dedication.

After the conclusion of the dedication festivities in Geneva we returned to Chicago on Tuesday, and from there my wife and I went directly to Red Wing, Minnesota, arriving there on May 16. In a letter to Pastor Cedarstam, dated May 17, I wrote, "Here we

---

[5] "The Scandinavians" were the Swedish and Norwegian members of the Synod of Northern Illinois. "The Americans" refers to the English-speaking members of the Synod, most of whom were supporters of S. S. Schmucker.

are now, without house and home, without goods, and almost without money, and to judge according to one's reason it seems dark indeed. There are many Swedish settlers here now and more are arriving daily. May the Lord give me grace to labor with all wisdom for the upbuilding of his kingdom."

The outlook was surely dark, and it is a wonder that we did not immediately lose courage and return to the place whence we had come. But the Lord strengthened us. In the first place, we could not get a house. There were not enough houses for the people in the town, and the houses they had were small and in poor condition. After trying for some time to find room somewhere, John Nilsson said to us, "I don't know of anything else for you to do than to move into my hog house for a while." He had just built a shed which he intended to use as a hog house but which had not yet been used for that purpose. We would likely have had to live in that hog house if a carpenter, Carl Anderson, had not permitted us to move into a very small bedroom in his little cottage for a few weeks.

On the following Sunday, which was Trinity Sunday, I preached my initial sermon in a partly finished store building. To conduct worship services standing by a counter in chips and shavings certainly was not inspiring, but when circumstances are compelling it is easy to disregard external surroundings. If there is real evidence of a genuine hunger and thirst for the Word of God, all the elements for a holy festivity are present. At the conclusion of the service subscriptions for the church building were received and a total of one hundred and four dollars was pledged. Fifty dollars had already been collected for this purpose. This was a good beginning for the new community.

The next Sunday, the First after Trinity, marked my first appearance as pastor in Vasa, which is located about twelve miles from Red Wing. The service was held in the home of Per Nilsson, who was known as "the rich man" because at that time he was the wealthiest person in the community. I was unaware of this fact as I preached my first sermon on the rich man and Lazarus. Had I known it, I would perhaps have been somewhat more circumspect in my remarks. But Nilsson was sensible enough to realize that my sermon was not a personal attack on him.

I shall now relate a few personal experiences from my ministry among the pioneers.

To entertain guests, for example, when there is no room for them to sleep is no simple matter. We have had such experiences several times this past summer and fall. On Sunday, June 29, when I returned to Red Wing, riding on a borrowed horse, I found the Rev. Mr. Esbjörn there. He was traveling about to collect money for the Scandinavian professorship. When he had preached in my stead both in the forenoon and in the afternoon and had secured some subscriptions, we set out for Vasa in the evening. The road was in poor condition, darkness fell, and Esbjörn was not much of a horseman. We agreed that he was to ride and I should lead the horse. Finally at midnight we came to a place where we had to leave the horse, and from there we had to walk the rest of the way to my home. Esbjörn was so tired, however, that he was compelled to lie down for a little while, so we lay down on a pile of fence posts and went to sleep. Later on in the night we awoke and continued our journey to my home, where the esteemed guest was joyfully received, but not without some qualms because of our extreme poverty. However, where there is room in the heart there will be room in the home, and our dear brother stayed with us for a whole week. During this time we visited most of the homes in the new settlement, and on the following Sunday Esbjörn preached a fine sermon on the transfiguration of Christ. Other visitors during the summer have been Pastors P. A. Cedarstam and Peter Carlson, whose fellowship has been most encouraging to me.

On July 6, shortly after Esbjörn's departure from Vasa, I received definite information regarding another settlement near Vasa, called Spring Garden. It happened thus: One Sunday morning just as I was preparing to conduct services, a yoke of oxen pulling a whole wagon load of people who were strangers in Vasa came toward us across the prairie from the south. Two families in this group each had a child that they wanted to have baptized. One of these families was that of Magnus Edstrom, and the other was that of John Wanberg. These people told me about their settlement and urged me to come to visit them as soon as possible. They had not known just where Vasa was, but they had set out to find the place and had driven many roundabout miles through the under-brush, over hills, and through valleys because they had heard that a Lutheran minister had come to Vasa.

On July 17 I made my first visit to Spring Garden, but it was no easy matter to find the place. I traveled about nine miles on foot. From White Rock to the Carl Häggström farm there is un-broken wilderness, and the traveler has to make his way in some places through a tangle of thorny bushes. One is fortunate, in-deed, to come through without tattered clothes. I once tore my clothing so badly that I had to get a number of pins to hold the rags together before I could show myself in public. I have made this trip several times during the summer. Worst of all is the rainy weather when one gets thoroughly soaked going through the bushes and tall grass. It has happened on occasion that while I have stood preaching the water ran off my clothing so that the floor was wet around me.

One very hot Sunday afternoon I had pushed my way through the underbrush to Spring Garden to hold services and conduct Holy Communion. At each end of the little house where we gathered there was a small window from which the sash had been removed in order to get better ventilation in the room. At one window a board nailed to the wall served as the communion table. On this crude table we had placed a bottle of wine and a plate with some pieces of bread.

Just as I began to preach the preparatory sermon an old hen flew in through the window, flapping her wings, and scattering the bits of bread all over the room. She landed on the floor in the midst of the congregation with a furious cackling as if she was possessed by Satan himself. How distracting this was to the decorum of the service may easily be imagined. When the hen had been thrown out and order again had been established, I resumed my sermon. But no sooner had I begun to preach than the old hen flew back in through the window and repeated her performance, only this time with more dire consequences, because she knocked the wine bottle to the floor, which fortunately did not break. Well, we finally learned our lesson and stationed a man outside the window to protect us from zealous hens.

My field of labor was constantly expanding. Soon I was making regular visits to the community of Cannon Falls, since a number of Scandinavian families have settled there during the summer. Most of my visits were made on foot because I did not yet own a horse. Meanwhile I had to think about providing a home for my wife and me. Accordingly I purchased the claim rights to one hundred sixty acres of land for one hundred and thirty dollars. On this land there was a very small log shack. It had a flat sod roof, a dirt floor, and no windows. Alongside this shack I built a shed of rough boards which were brought from Red Wing, fifteen miles away, in two oxcart loads. As soon as the walls were up we moved into our palace, without roof, door, or windows. The mattress was filled with hay and laid on a pile of shavings, and there we slept peacefully the first night under the protecting hand of God. When my wife shook out the mattress the next morning she found a snake in the hay. There were plenty of snakes around.

Next day we made both ceiling and roof by stretching cloth over the top of the walls. On the plain board walls we put wall paper, and on the floor, which was a patchwork of odds and ends of lumber, we laid a cheap carpet which we had brought with us from Indiana. Thus we provided for ourselves an elegant home which had, however, one failing, namely, that it did not keep out the rain. We had to sleep, therefore, under an umbrella on rainy nights. We fashioned a table and some chairs by boring holes in some pieces of lumber and inserting wooden pins to serve as legs. Decked out with some bright cloth on table and chairs our furniture looked very good. "How elegant you have it," said our neighbor Hans Mattson as he looked in on us one day. My wife invited him to stay for a cup of coffee, and as he sat drinking his coffee the homemade chair went to pieces and with a crash he fell backwards to the floor. There was no harm done, however, and we all had a good laugh at our elegant poverty.

We have fared well enough in our modest little home, but life would have been somewhat more pleasant if we had had enough to eat. Our food supplies have often been very meager. It is almost impossible to forage for food in the surrounding countryside, and it is fifteen miles to the nearest town. Furthermore, there has been so little money with which to buy anything. We have lived one day at a time, and God has graciously provided for our necessities. It has been particularly difficult for my wife to be isolated in the wilderness by herself while I have had to be absent from home for protracted periods.

Our neighbors have been in the same circumstances as we, and no one has been able to help his neighbor very much. Our nearest neighbor, Jacob Rasmussen, who lives a little more than a mile north of us, arrived here about the same time we did. He and his family came from Pecatonica, Illinois, crossing the state of Wisconsin with oxen. Among other useful articles that he brought with him was a loom, which he used as his first shelter. He set it up on the ground, covered it with quilts and rags, and so provided a place where his family could crawl in and sleep at night.

He soon dug a cave-like cellar in the hillside and hung a quilt over the opening. When any visitors come to the place, his little daughters usually dart quickly into the cave like little ground squirrels scurrying into their burrows.

In the latter part of August we have had the pleasure of having as our guest Dr. William A. Passavant from Pittsburgh, Pennsylvania. We were happy to have him with us, but were not a little perplexed as to how we would be able to care for him in the midst of our limited circumstances. However, things went better than we had feared. He was, of course, permitted to occupy our one and only bed. But, unfortunately, it rained one night and the roof leaked. It is no wonder, therefore, that he dreamed that he lay at the bottom of a lake in great anguish. This was his first trip to Minnesota.

Spiritual conditions in this area at the close of the year 1856 have not been very encouraging. Very few people give evidence of any genuine spirituality, and even where there has been some interest shown in getting a congregation established, this concern has often been stifled by indifference and by the financial expenses involved in such an undertaking. When the first wave of curiosity has been spent, people are reluctant to attend services, and no one wants to submit to discipline. There have been certain ones, officers of the congregation, who have even wanted to have the pastor along at their card games and drinking parties, and they seem to have the idea that everything here ought to be exactly as it was in old Sweden. Furthermore, the minds of the people are constantly troubled with worries regarding economic security.

The salary that the congregations have been able to pay me this past year has amounted to approximately two hundred dollars in cash and some produce. This, together with seventy-five dollars additional support from the Lutheran Home Mission Society, has certainly been an inadequate stipend. It would be wrong to try to make anyone believe that a minister can live on three hundred dollars a year, even with the strictest economy, especially when he has to furnish his own house and horse and wagon. The inevitable result is that one has to go into debt if credit is available, or otherwise try to earn the necessities of life by manual labor.

On October 1 I made a trip to Illinois to attend the conference meeting in Galesburg and the synodical convention in Dixon. When I reached Mendota, Illinois, I met the Rev. Erland Carlsson, the Rev. A. Andreen, and a new pastor recently arrived from Sweden, the Rev. Jonas Swensson, who is at present located in Sugar Grove, Pennsylvania. He made a good impression on me.

We continued on our journey to Galesburg and there we met the Rev. L. P. Esbjörn, the Rev. T. N. Hasselquist, the Rev. M. F. Hokanson, the Rev. P. A. Cedarstam, the Rev. B. G. Bergenlund, and two newcomers from Sweden. One was A. R. Cervin, who for some reason struck me as being so educated that I was afraid of him. I soon learned, however, that there was no danger, for his education was a real adornment to his character. He possesses a heart filled with fervent love for the Lord Jesus Christ and for the brethren, and he has an earnest zeal for the work of the kingdom of God. The other newcomer was the Rev. O. C. T. Andreen, a deeply religious man. In his presence, though he was little both physically and in his own estimation, one felt very small. "This is a holy man, a sanctified soul," was the thought that crossed my mind when I met him.[6]

We went directly from this inspiring meeting to the synodical convention in Dixon. This meeting was especially memorable for some of us in that we were here ordained into the holy ministry. It is customary in the Synod of Northern Illinois to ordain a man after he has been licensed to function as a pastor for a year or

[6] The Mississippi Conference met at Galesburg, Illinois, October 2-4, 1856. For a translation of the minutes of this meeting see *Augustana Historical Society Publications*, Vol. X, pp. 109 f.

two and has proved himself worthy of the ministerial calling. There were four of us who were ordained, namely, G. A. Bowers, P. A. Cedarstam, A. Andreen, and myself. Our ordination gave us greater certainty in our calling, a certainty that is greatly needed in the many trials which come to those who serve in the holy ministry.[7]

In December, after a considerable amount of snow had fallen and the countryside lay in the deep grip of winter, my wife and I, together with our friend Jonas Engberg, made a trip to Cannon Falls, Minnesota, where I conducted services. We rode in a small, low, wooden sleigh pulled by a frail, little pony. On our return trip we lost our way in a driving snowstorm. There was nothing to do but to leave my wife in the sleigh as Engberg and I walked in opposite directions trying to locate the trail. We had to be extremely careful not to get too far apart and thus be lost in the blizzard, so we kept calling to each other now and then. Finally we had to get down on our hands and knees in the snow and feel with our hands for the tracks in the frozen earth. At last we were fortunate to find the trail, and we continued on our way home.

[7] The meeting of the Synod of Northern Illinois was held in Dixon, Illinois, October 8-13, 1856. An abstract of the minutes of this convention is given in *ibid.*, pp. 32 ff.

MISSIONARY JOURNEY TO THE WEST COAST[1]

1885-1886

October 1, 1885. I departed from my home this day after bidding my family farewell. Bought a ticket for half price to Moorhead for $4.60 via the Northern Pacific Railroad. I sat up all night, and reached Moorhead about 8:30 A.M. on Friday, October 2. Have had a good trip so far. Here in Moorhead I have stayed in the home of the Rev. John O. Cavallin, pastor of the Swedish Lutheran church. I have met a number of old acquaintances and have purchased several small items for my trip west.

October 4, St. Michael's Sunday. This day I preached in the Swedish Lutheran church here. It has been very cold and the attendance at services was small.

October 5. At 3:45 A.M. I left Moorhead. I bought a ticket for Wallula Junction, Washington, at half price for $42.40. I bade farewell to Brother Cavallin, who has shown me such generous Christian hospitality. The most important towns west of Fargo, North Dakota, are Tower City, Valley City, Jamestown, Sanborn, Bismarck, and Mandan. Montana is a land of mountains like the

[1] From October, 1885, to May, 1886, Eric Norelius undertook an extensive journey to the west coast as traveling missionary for the Augustana Synod. The object of this journey was to inspect the work which the Synod had already started on the west coast and to seek out new Swedish settlements, where congregations might be established in the future. The pages that follow record some of Norelius' experiences during this missionary journey.

Alps, excepting a small portion of the eastern section of the state. The scenery is absolutely indescribable and has a strange and exhilarating effect upon me. O the majesty and glory of God, creator of heaven and earth!

October 6. At 8:40 A.M. we crossed the Yellowstone River and approached Billings, Montana, a busy little city which has a population of about two thousand people. The buildings here are mostly of brick and stone. The city of Billings lies in a river valley, with bluffs rising on either side as high as some four hundred feet. I had a good breakfast in Billings, as much as I could eat for seventy-five cents. This is indeed a royal life!

Soon after leaving Billings I caught my first sight of the white-clad peaks of the Snow Mountains. What a thrilling sight to behold the snow peaks bathed in sunshine and yet so high that the snow does not melt. The closer we came to the range of the Snow Mountains the more majestic they appeared. Scattered throughout the broad foothills are a number of sprawling cattle ranches. The scenery is constantly changing; it is surely a feast for the eyes. Here and there a little prairie dog sticks his head up from his burrow and barks at the passing train. At one point I caught sight of a large wolf standing on a bluff watching the train go by.

Presently we came to Big Timber. What a glorious sight lies before us! The great river which we have been following loses itself among the high bluffs and foothills up ahead. Far to the south, snow-capped peaks reach for the sky. Soon there is a fork in the river with towering mountains forming the crotch. Never in all my life have I seen anything to compare with this.

At about 1:15 in the afternoon we reached Livingston. Here the railroad leaves the Yellowstone River as the stream turns southward and pushes its way through a narrow gorge in the hills. We now began to climb toward higher levels. Two great locomotives are necessary to bring the train over the high mountain pass.

At Hopper's Station we met trains number one and two, and just beyond this point we entered a tunnel which is more than a mile long. As we emerged from the tunnel we started down a long slope toward the Gallatin River. All around us was a dense and beautiful pine forest, and here and there in the mountains there are evidences of mining operations. As we approached the Gallatin Valley we passed the military post, Fort Ellis. The valley with its towering mountains on either side is fertile and productive. Farms with lush fields are scattered throughout the area.

Down the valley a way we came to Bozeman. The town itself is situated some distance from the railroad station. As we continue through the valley we follow along the Gallatin River, and toward dusk we arrived at Helena. Here the dining cars and one passenger car were left behind as we began a steep climb up into the mountain range. I stood on the platform and watched the unfolding panorama until we reached the high point in the pass and began our descent on the other side of the range. It is a shame that one must waste time in bed sleeping when there is so much to see.

October 7. We passed through Missoula about dawn today. We are following Clark's Fork westward, and in the vicinity of Eddy I caught sight of an encampment of Flathead Indians. This entire areas is covered with a dense growth of pine trees. The water in the Clark River seems almost as green as the surrounding trees, as it rushes through narrow gorges and dashes against great boulders in its swift way to the lower valley. As we approach the Montana-Idaho border the scenery is wild and majestic. The little town of Heron lies on the border between the two states. Here there is a three-story hotel called "Mountain House."

The town of Heron is comprised of about thirty small wooden shanties, most of which appear to be saloons. And now we are in Idaho. As we pass Clark's Fork Station we are about as far north as we shall go. Along the tracks grow bushes that look like some species of boxelder, bearing a berry fruit of light blue color. Here and there among the pines one can see some birch, cottonwood, and elm trees. As we reach Kootenay and Sand Point, the river widens until it becomes a veritable lake. A steamboat is making its way across the expanse of water, while a woman sits at the open door of her cabin reading a book without casting a glimpse at the magnificent scene spread out before her. At Sand Point we leave the Clark River and cross a sandy plain heading for Spokane Falls in Washington Territory.

At Idaho Line Station we cross over the border into Washington Territory. Here the country seems less arid and wild. Farms and grain fields, even some acres of corn, are scattered here and there. The weather is superb, and the air is exceedingly light and stimulating. Spokane Falls is already quite a ctiy, with broad streets and a prosperous appearance. At Spokane Falls we leave the mountains behind us and enter a broad expanse of rolling, sandy prairie land, overgrown with sage brush and bunch grass. This country is ideal pasture land for cattle. Here and there strange looking rock formations rise high above the ground like tall sentinels. The rolling land stretches out toward the far horizon as far as the eye can see. Now and then one catches a glimpse of grazing herds of cattle and sheep, and of small settlements where livestock feeding and shipping seem to be the main business. Close to the town of Sprague there is a sizeable lake, several miles long and about a mile wide. Rocky cliffs are scattered along the banks of the lake. As the sun sets on the western horizon we are told that we are approaching the Columbia River.

October 8. I arose a little before four o'clock this morning, just in time to see the little town of Dallen in the first light of dawn as our train passed through the settlement. The scenery here is absolutely indescribable. Between Viento and Wyeth there are immense mountain peaks, tremendous gorges, deep forests, and winding through it all is the mighty Columbia River. The weather is as beautiful as a summer day. The trees and foliage are green, fresh, and colorful. I had a good breakfast at Bonneville, which is forty-nine miles from Portland. Before reaching Bonneville we passed Cascade Lake. What a magnificent sight the river gives as it struggles to push its way through the mountains, dashing spray high into the air as the hurtling water strikes the mighty boulders which lie in the midst of the river bed. The government is undertaking a very great project here in the building of a railroad bridge across the river.

Soon after leaving Bonneville we come to Multnomah Falls, consisting of an upper and lower fall descending from a height of 884 feet. Within a short while two other falls are to be seen in the distance. Our train arrives in East Portland, where we transfer to a steamship which takes us across the Willamette River to Portland.

We reached Portland about 10:10 in the forenoon, and there on the dock to meet me was the Rev. J. W. Skans, pastor of Immanuel Lutheran church in Portland. I appreciated his thoughtfulness, for now I did not need to worry about finding my way in a strange city. We went immediately to his home.

Portland is a large and thriving city with wide streets and excellent stores and shops. It is situated on the west bank of the Willamette River and stretches both north and south for several miles, while to the west it reaches up into the towering bluffs. The entire city is surrounded by a dense pine forest. To the east is the Cascade mountain range, with Mt. Hood dominating the landscape with its snow-covered peak.

I was heartily welcomed in the home of the Rev. Mr. Skans. His family includes his wife and a three-year-old son. I was now informed that the Rev. L. O. Lindh of La Conner, Washington, and the Rev. Jacob Hoikka of Astoria, Oregon, were expected to arrive today. They arrived in the afternoon.

In the evening a service of worship was held in the undercroft of the church. I preached the sermon using as my text a portion of Acts 16, which deals with the conversion of Lydia. Not many attended the service, but those who were there seemed to be attentive. In conversation with the brethren I was given information regarding conditions on the west coast and the future prospects for our missionary program in this area.

October 9. The weather is variable. It rains for a while and then clears, followed before long by more rain. I feel fine today. Went downtown for a visit to a Chinese festival. The street of the Chinese quarter was bedecked with Chinese lanterns, colored balloons, and paper decorations of all kinds. We went into a three-storied Chinese temple filled with gewgaws and several hideous looking idols. The walls were covered with pictures, placards, and tinsel, while in every room there were burning candles, smoking incense, and throngs of laughing, talking Chinese people. We postponed further investigation of the Chinese festival and proceeded instead to the Mechanics and Agricultural Fair of Oregon. I was not much interested in the mechanical exhibits. But the agricultural exhibits proved to be fascinating. I have never in my life seen such wheat and oats, such fruits, including apples, pears, and grapes, such vegetables, including turnips, cabbage, and cauliflower. The people out here seem to be just as decent and respectable as anywhere else.

October 10. Today the weather is wonderful. Have not been able to see Mt. Hood because of the clouds, but this afternoon for the first time I beheld that majestic peak. I have never seen anything more regal. In the afternoon, Skans, Hoikka, and I returned to the Chinese festival for a second visit. There was a very large crowd in that section of the city. We entered the temple, which in broad daylight seemed drab and dingy. In one large room there was an altar filled with incense burners. Above the altar were a number of idols, both pictures and life-sized statues. Chinese people, laughing and jabbering while they smoked long cheroots, were wandering about the premises looking at the idol figures and various other displays of art work. A Chinese in ordinary clothes had charge of the incense burning.

We climbed a winding staircase to the upper story, and here, too, the rooms were filled with pictures and figures of idols and gewgaws of all descriptions. The strange smell of incense filled the entire house. In one corner of the upper story there was a balcony where a company of Chinese musicians played constantly during the festivities. But such music! One man beat upon a small cymbal, which sounded exactly like the clang of an empty frying pan. Another scraped on a kind of violin with two or three strings, while another pounded a huge gong.

Out on the street the highlight of the festival was under way. A plain table had been placed in the street half surrounded by five small altar tables upon each of which the image of an idol had been placed. There were also incense burners, lighted candles, together with a sheaf of brown paper upon which, it was said, the trespasses of the people were listed. This section of the street was closed to all traffic by the police. Presently three Chinese priests appeared dressed in red robes and black hats, with Chinese letters embroidered on the back of their gowns. Following the priests came five boys who were the acolytes, each carrying a small idol.

The priests proceeded to the center table, and the acolytes lined up behind them. A musician, playing an instrument which looked like a clarinet, sat at one end of the table. And now the ritual began. The priests and acolytes bowed deeply in all directions and the music began, while another musician, farther back, struck a large gong several times. Meanwhile the priest on the right began a rhythmic beat on a small drum as an accompaniment to a weird sort of chant which the other two priests now began. Presently the priests sat down before the table and continued the chant for about forty-five minutes, all the while accompanied by the strange instruments. After this part of the ceremony was concluded the priests arose and began a procession around the altar and the tables, bowing very low before each idol image, and followed by the acolytes who imitated every priestly gesture. Though this was undoubtedly a very solemn ceremony, to us it seemed almost laughable and ridiculous. Finally, the strips of brown paper were burned, while a couple of attendants emerged from the temple with a large linen cloth in which they placed all the idol images from the altar and tables and carried them back into the temple precincts. And so the Chinese festival was concluded. While the long and tedious ceremony had been in progress, the Chinese audience was standing around laughing, talking, and smoking, apparently enjoying the spectacle quite as much as their inquisitive and curious white visitors. Here one had opportunity to witness the true spirit of paganism. O God, how degraded man can become! But is the paganism of the white man essentially different or better than the Asiatic idolatry?

October 11. On this Sunday Brother Hoikka preached and I conducted the liturgy at the forenoon service. There were about fifty or sixty people in attendance. The weather is clear, but I have been comfortable with my overcoat on. The high humidity in this climate aggravates my catarrh, and besides, people do not heat their homes adequately out here.

In the evening I preached at the vesper service, using as my text Matthew 9:22. I spoke about man's sin and our salvation in Jesus Christ. We administered Holy Communion to about thirty people. When I arrived back at the Skans home I felt unusually tired.

October 12. Today I feel much better than I did yesterday. I have made the acquaintance of the local Norwegian pastor, the Rev. Mr. Engh, a member of the Norwegian Synod. He seems to be a fine man. Spent most of the day in my room writing letters.

October 13. Thy grace, O Lord, is new every morning. Praised be thy name. Weather today is cloudy, but the temperature is like summer. I have met a certain Gust Holms and his wife. They are visiting here and live in Astoria, Oregon. They are of the opinion that this part of the country will never become a productive farming area. Nor do they know of any particular concentration of Swedish settlers on the west coast. They are of the opinion that the Scandinavian settlements are scattered all over the west and that the immigrants are being absorbed by other groups. Today I wrote my first article about my western trip for the synodical journal *Augustana* and sent it off in the mail.

October 14. I rested well last night. The nights are really chilly out here. It was foggy until about ten o'clock this forenoon, but it cleared off and the rest of the day was bright and pleasant.

This afternoon I accompanied the Rev. Mr. Skans to a sewing society meeting where about ten women were gathered. They were fat and not particularly interesting.

This evening I attended a meeting of the young people of the congregation. I spoke to them about the characteristic differences which are inculcated in the minds of people by the three major denominations, namely, the Roman Catholic, the Reformed,[2] and the Lutheran. There were about a dozen present. I think something could be accomplished with these young people.

October 16. Another beautiful day. I left Portland at 11:45 in the forenoon, bound for Tacoma via the Northern Pacific Railroad. Forty miles below Portland we crossed the Columbia River on a very large ferry, landing at Kalama. At several points between Portland and Kalama the three great peaks, Mt. Hood, Mt. Helens, and Mt. Tacoma were clearly visible. During the trip I met two Swedish settlers who are located in Silver Lake, Washington Territory. They said that several other Swedish families live there. I got the distinct impression, however, that these people are very dull

---

[2] "Reformed" here is a general term meaning "Protestants" other than Lutherans.

and altogether distinterested in anything churchly or religious. They have been on the west coast about fifteen years and thrive in this climate. Because the Swedish settlements are so widely scattered it will be almost impossible to do anything with them as far as the church is concerned. Their speech, too, has become almost an unintelligible mixture of Swedish and English.

When we reached Silver Lake my new-found acquaintances got off the train. Before they left, however, I asked them how they, who had been brought up in the productive province of Gotland, Sweden, could feel at home out here in this wilderness country. To this query one of them replied, "When a fellow has a full stomach, some good whiskey, and a cooperative wife, he can feel at home anywhere."

Toward evening I arrived in Tacoma, where I met a certain Albert Turner, who directed me to the home of his brother John, who in turn showed me the way to the residence of the Rev. G. A. Anderson, pastor of the Swedish Lutheran congregation in Tacoma. I was heartily welcomed in the Anderson home, and my host gave me his own bed for the night.

October 18. On this Sunday the weather is beautiful and mild. It has been a great joy to go to the little Swedish Lutheran church here in Tacoma for worship. The church, which was built in 1883, seats about 250 people. We first attended the Sunday school hour. Only a few children were present. At the service of worship the Rev. Mr. Anderson preached the sermon for the Twentieth Sunday after Trinity. I conducted the liturgical service. There were about fifty people in attendance. It seems that Sunday morning services are not very well attended out here on the west coast.

In the evening I preached the sermon, using as my text Hebrews 10:19. There were a few more present than at the morning service.

October 19. This is another beautiful day. Great is thy goodness and mercy, O Lord! What is man that thou art mindful of him?

This day my host, the Rev. Mr. Anderson, received notice from his landlady that he could no longer take his meals at the rooming house but would be permitted to keep his room. We have, therefore, been eating at the restaurant, limiting ourselves to two meals a day. A restaurant meal in this city costs twenty-five cents for as much as one can eat. Most of this day has been spent writing letters.

October 20. The beautiful weather continues, and the climate here is so salubrious that every bone in this old body rejoices. As I arose this morning the old aches and pains were practically gone.

This afternoon, John Turner, a member of the local congregation, took us for a ride throughout the city for about two hours. He drove a fine team of blacks. We went first to the so-called "old city," about two miles from the loop in Tacoma. The old city marks the original Tacoma settlement. It is now a ward in the larger city precincts. There is a large sawmill in the old town, with a huge furnace which is constantly ablaze with scrap from the mill. Alongside the mill is a wharf where a half-dozen ships are anchored while they are loaded with lumber. One ship, we were told, is bound for Hong Kong with both lumber and a number of Chinese passengers. Many Chinese work in the sawmill; they have their drab living quarters at the foot of the bluff near the mill. White laborers earn about thirty dollars a month; the Chinese get much less.

The oldest church in Tacoma is located in the old city. It is an Episcopal chapel, a small shanty built at the base of a giant fir tree which measures some five or six feet in diameter. The giant fir has been cut about thirty feet above ground, and here on top of the thirty-foot stump the church bell has been hung. Someone remarked, "Here is a bell-tower which is at least a hundred and fifty years old."

From the old city we drove on up the Puyallup Valley, some three or four miles from the city. Here the native Indians have erected a large public school under Roman Catholic and Presbyterian auspices. These Indians are civilized and dress and live like white people. There are said to be only a very few full-blooded Indians left in this area. Many of the early settlers took Indian wives, and the half-breed Indians seem to be a very sturdy people. The greater portion of Puyallup Valley is populated by white farmers who raise large crops of hops and beans.

After returning to the city, we had supper at Mr. Luft's restaurant for twenty-five cents apiece. Mr. Luft is a Swede, born in Stockholm, and before coming out here he spent several years in California.

In the evening we had services in the Swedish Lutheran church. I preached the sermon, using as my text II Corinthians 5:1-15. There were about twenty people in attendance. I also met the German Lutheran pastor, the Rev. L. Wolf, of the Joint Synod of Ohio, who seemed to be a lovable brother. He serves a small congregation of about twenty-five communicants, who meet each week in our Swedish church building.

October 21. Praise God for a good night's rest and for renewed health and strength! I feel fresh and light as a feather today. I have just read a newspaper dispatch from Ishpeming, Michigan, which reports a snowfall there of eight inches, which has stalled all traffic, including the trains. What a contrast between here and there! We had a good breakfast at the restaurant for twenty-five cents, which included grapes, porksteak, and coffee. I began preparations for my trip to Seattle.

At 1 P.M. Pastor Anderson and I boarded the steamship "Messenger." The scenery is superb. We arrived in Seattle about 4 P.M. The first thing we did in Seattle was to look up a good restaurant and get something to eat.

After mealtime we made our way to the Swedish Lutheran church, which is beautifully situated here in Seattle. It gives a better appearance and impression than our churches in Portland

and Tacoma. It is a good deal larger. I believe I could get along well here, if there were enough people to work with. Toward evening we made our way to an out-of-the-way part of town called Union Lake, where we looked up a widow named Mrs. Alstad, who with her brother operates a rooming house and a small grocery store. They seem like good and pious folk. They have a very comfortable and pleasant place. Here we secured lodging for the night.

October 22. I have decided to stay in Seattle for the next three Sundays and bargained with Mrs. Alstad for lodging at a cost of five dollars a week. Thereupon we called on a number of Swedish families, all of whom seemed to be indifferent to church and religion. Also called on the Swedish vice-consul, Mr. Kihlberg, and his brother, both of whom are indifferent to religion and completely engrossed in their business affairs.

We had our noon meal with Mrs. Alstad, after which the Rev. Mr. Anderson started for Port Madison to visit some Swedish families residing there. We agreed that we should conduct a Reformation festival in Tacoma on the evening of November 9. I wrote letters to my son Sigfrid, the Rev. Mr. Lindholm, the Rev. Mr. Cedarstam, and a long article for Dr. Passavant for publication in the *Workman*.[3]

October 23. This evening I preached for the first time in Seattle. There were about twelve people in attendance. The prospects for a thriving congregation in Seattle do not appear to be very bright. There are, to be sure, a good number of our countrymen residing here, but almost all of them seem to be entirely indifferent to everything spiritual and churchly, and a good many are downright antagonistic and openly opposed to religion, especially to our Lutheran church. A number of our people have ap-

---

[3] The *Workman* was a bi-weekly church paper founded by W. A. Passavant in Pittsburgh and edited by him from 1880 until his death in 1894. Through the pages of this paper Passavant promoted the missionary and eleemosynary causes in which he was interested.

parently been infected with agnosticism, and others have espoused sectarianism. No one seems to be concerned about our Lutheran church. One can hardly claim that we have an organized congregation here. One of the trustees once came to church dead drunk and caused a terrible uproar; two others have moved away from the city. A certain Nilsson, a tailor, seems to be the only person with the slightest concern for our congregation. He has been serving as both treasurer and janitor, but even he has very little interest in our affairs. There is no organist. A girl belonging to the Norwegian Methodist church has been persuaded to play for the service a few times, but since she has received no remuneration she has refused to continue. This evening she was not present, and I suppose she will not show up again. It looks dark indeed. If anything is to be accomplished in Seattle it will be necessary to station here a diligent, patient, and gifted pastor who will work unceasingly among the people.

October 25. This is Sunday. O Lord, fill my heart with thy light and love! This is a cloudy day with intermittent rain falling. I conducted services in the Swedish Lutheran church, preaching on the text Matthew 7:27-31 to about twenty-five people. We had no organist, and therefore I had to line out the hymns myself. I was grateful when at least one woman came to me and bade me welcome to Seattle and expressed her gratitude for the privilege of hearing God's Word. Otherwise she and my landlady are the only ones who have shown any real interest in religion or extended to me any Christian friendliness.

In the evening I held a service and preached to some twenty-five people, using as my text Isaiah 55:1-3. My rooming house is located about a mile from the church, and it is miserable and tiring to trudge that distance in the mud and rain. I felt very downhearted this evening, and it was not easy to preach. There was not, I fear, much blessing in my sermon tonight, even though the text was a glorious word of truth. After the service I sloshed back to my room, tired and depressed. O how cold in spiritual matters it seems to be in this place!

October 26. O Lord, thy grace endureth from generation to generation! Again I am permitted to celebrate my birthday anniversary. For fifty-two years I have been privileged to dwell on this earth. It is surely a wonder that the son whom my mother brought into the world fifty-two years ago should this day find himself away out on the Pacific coast, many thousands of miles away from the quiet little farm home in the Swedish province of Helsingland.

The day was overcast when I arose early this morning, but it has since cleared. I have received several birthday greetings in the mail, including those from my wife and my sons, Leonard, Sigfrid, and Theodore. This gladdened my heart. Today I met an elderly Norwegian by the name of Larsen, who came here from Freeborn County, Minnesota. He is not happy out here, nor is he satisfied with the spiritual and religious conditions in this part of the country.

October 27. More cloudy and foggy weather. Today I have not been feeling well. I seem to have a distressing ache in my legs, hands, and feet. I am depressed. It has been raining intermittently almost all day. I am beginning to think that this wet and chilly weather may not agree with me in the long run.

October 30. I awoke today with a strange heaviness in my head. At dawn the skies were dark with heavy clouds, but during the forenoon the sun broke through the overcast. I have been out in the city seeking Swedish families. I found a Mrs. Charles Johnson from Ljusdal in Helsingland. She does not feel well here in Seattle. Her husband hails from the province of Westmanland, Sweden. They lived for a time in Minneapolis, Minnesota, before coming to the west coast. Their dwelling place is little more than a miserable shanty located on a swampy lot. They have no church connections, although they would like to belong to some congregation. The man impressed me as being a very unreliable character. I also visited an elderly Norwegian family by the name of Larsen. They have a fairly decent house near the Norwegian Methodist church. They also own a forty-acre farm about six miles from Madland, which cost them eleven hundred dollars. They are not happy out here, and would move away if they could sell their holdings profitably. They do not belong to any congregation, although they seem to be pious and respectable people.

October 31. I awakened with a heavy head. Another rainy and chilly day. I do not feel well in this kind of weather. I yearn to leave this place, especially in view of the fact that I do not seem to be able to accomplish anything here. No one has sought me out for consultation, and not a person has invited me to stay on and continue the work here. I have never been in a more disagreeable place in all my life.

November 1, All Saints' Day. It is cloudy and chilly. At divine service this forenoon I preached to a congregation of about twenty-five people. I had hoped to see a larger attendance, but it is difficult to awaken any religious interest here.

I was invited for dinner and supper to the Larsens', the Norwegian family residing near the Methodist church. In the evening we held a Reformation service, at which about sixty or seventy people were present. This is the largest audience I have had since coming out here. I trudged home in the darkness, feeling tired and ill.

November 8. I did not sleep well last night. Some three hundred soldiers arrived in town during the night for the purpose of controlling the people who are said to be ready to attack the Chinese. This is the interpretation given by Governor Squires. He has much property here in Seattle and wants the Chinese laborers to remain here. He claims that the anti-Chinese sentiment in Seattle and Tacoma threatens to break into open violence and has therefore called in the Sixth Company of the National Guard to both Seattle and Tacoma. This is ridiculous. As far as Seattle is concerned, there has been some anti-Chinese agitation, but nothing that threatens to become violence. It is only after the soldiers arrived that there has been any threat of open hostilities against the Chinese. Early today a couple of soldiers clipped the pigtails off a Chinese worker, while some other soldiers threw another Chinese into the water just as he was going on board a ship leaving Seattle. The presence of soldiers here under these false pretenses will surely cause a violent uproar. In Tacoma there is greater danger of violence. There, I understand, a whole colony of Chinese workers was driven out of town, several Chinese homes were burned, and some Chinese were brutally beaten.

This being the Twenty-third Sunday after Trinity I held a service in our church this forenoon. I based my sermon on Psalm 23. About a dozen people attended. The Larsen family invited me again for dinner. At three o'clock in the afternoon we held a communion service in the church. Six women and two men, a total of eight souls, were present. Of these all were Norwegians except three women. Work among the Norwegians seems to have brighter prospects than among the Swedish people.

This evening at 7:30 I conducted my final service here in Seattle, and for me it was a melancholy and painful experience. When I entered the church I found there a group of rowdies, both boys and girls, who jeered at me and, laughing among themselves, tried to make it impossible to hold our meeting. They were here to take matters into their own hands. I asked God to help me be calm and to meet these young ruffians in the proper way. I first lined out a hymn, read a portion of the first chapter of the Gospel of John, led the assembly in prayer, announced another hymn, and then preached the sermon. It was clearly apparent that the evil spirit of agnosticism was present in the chapel, for as I was speaking one after another of those present got up and walked out. Even Mr. Peterson the tailor left the meeting. When I first came into the church, Peterson was sitting playing and practicing the organ. When I asked him to play for the service he refused. He sat quietly and listened to my sermon for a while, and then began to grow restless, and finally simply got up and walked out while I was speaking. My heart went out to these wretched people because I had not spoken harshly to them but had sought to show them the way to Jesus, who is the merciful Savior of us all. Our mission in Seattle does not look hopeful.

It had not rained all day, but just as I was about to leave the church after service it began to pour. It was muddy, wet, and cold. A man named Lumke had the courtesy to accompany me and help me carry my luggage downtown. I stopped at the Brunswick House hotel for the night in order to catch the boat for Tacoma early in the morning. I paid seventy-five cents for room and breakfast, but the place was infested with bedbugs, so I had a very uncomfortable night. It rained until morning.

November 9. It has rained all night and has continued during the entire forenoon. I boarded the steamboat "Zephyr" at 7:30 this morning bound for Tacoma. It was with a real sense of relief that I left Seattle, since I was so depressed in that city. I am thankful, however, for the privilege of bringing a witness on behalf of my Lord Jesus Christ to these people, speaking to them about the great issues of life and death. I am deeply sorry, however, that I have seen so little fruit of my visit in Seattle. But perhaps some good will come of it, particularly among the Norwegians. Farewell, Seattle, I will doubtless never see you again, nor do I desire that I shall ever again in this life return under circumstances which prevail at the present time!

I arrived in Tacoma just after the noon hour. Ate my lunch at Luft's restaurant. I met the Rev. Mr. Anderson and went with him to his rooming house, where we stayed until it was time to go to church for the Reformation festival. The meeting began at 7:30 P.M., and I delivered the Reformation address. A good many people were in attendance at this service. At the conclusion of the festival Brother Anderson and I went to the Western Hotel, close to the railroad depot, and rented a room for the night. A company of soldiers was camped outside the hotel. They were there, as in Seattle, to "protect" the Chinese from violence. It is reported that the police have arrested a number of Tacoma residents for participating in riots against the Chinese.

November 10. We had a fairly restful night. We arose early and took the train at 5:30 A.M. for Portland. We had breakfast in Tenino. Arrived in Portland about 1:30 this afternoon. At the home of the Rev. Mr. Skans I met Brother Peter Carlson.

November 12. This is a beautiful day. The Rev. L. O. Lindh from La Conner, Washington, together with L. Hokenson, postmaster at Elim, Washington, are here. In the evening a Reformation service was held. The church was tastefully decorated for the occasion. On the wall over the pulpit there was a large picture of Luther with the words "The just shall live by faith." The Rev. Peter Carlson opened tbe service with Scripture reading and prayer. The Rev. Mr. Anderson gave a talk on the predecessors of the Reformation, and I delivered an address on Luther as God's instrument for the renewal of the church. The congregation sang well, and on the whole the service was successful. An offering was received amounting to twenty dollars.

November 13. This day we held a special district meeting. We made a list of mission stations in this northwest region and found that there were seven of them. We decided upon a program of visitations to these mission stations. We also agreed that we could not recommend for licensure Mr. John Mellgren, a lay evangelist who has been working in the vicinity of Bear Creek, Idaho. We also discussed the Chinese and labor questions. I gave forty dollars to Brother Skans, asking him to keep it for me until further notice.

November 15. This is Sunday. The weather is beautiful. I preached today at both the morning and the evening services.

There were a good many people in attendance. The offering at the evening service amounted to ten dollars.

November 17. Today it is cloudy with intermittent rain. This morning Brother Carlson and I bade Pastor Skans farewell and left Portland about 7:30 A.M. bound for Marshfield. I left my heavy baggage at the Skans home. Carlson and I traveled for half-fare, and our destination was Draines, about a hundred and fifty miles from Portland, via the Oregon and California Railroad. We passed through Salem, the capital city of Oregon. Salem is beautifully situated, with a number of fine buildings. The capitol building is attractive but not particularly impressive. The city is surrounded by a dense forest. One catches occasional glimpses of the Cascade and the Coast ranges of mountains. We arrived in Draines a little after four o'clock in the afternoon. The best hotel was none too good, and our room for the night cost one dollar.

November 18. We traveled by stage to Scottsburg, thirty-six miles from Draines. A windstorm which struck the area yesterday had blown down a number of trees across the road halting all traffic. We were therefore compelled to ride in a lumber wagon about a mile and a half down the road where the stage awaited us on the other side of the fallen trees. It was a miserable, jolting ride, seated as we were on a couple of boards thrown across the wagon box. We found the stage much more comfortable. The stage route follows the Elker Creek through the mountains. At one point the road makes a ten mile curve through a high pass, which is more than a thousand feet in elevation. In the middle of this curve three large trees were blown down across the road, and we were all obliged to get out and help clear the way. After helping to chop and lift the heavy tree limbs, I climbed up a mountain slope to get a view of the countryside, but the exertion was too much, and I began to feel ill, but recovered after a while. Fortunately the weather was almost ideal, so that our trip, in spite of the inconveniences, was in general a pleasant experience. About sundown we reached Scottsburg, a small town nestled between towering mountains. We spent the night in the Palmer House Hotel, which happened to be a rather pleasant place. Our room cost one dollar.

November 19. We departed from Scottsburg in the morning and traveled by steamboat twenty miles downstream on the Elker River to Gardiner, where we landed about ten o'clock in the forenoon. Gardiner is a small town with houses that are freshly painted and yards that are green and colorful. It has a population of about two hundred and fifty people. The only business establishment in town is a sawmill. There is a Baptist church here, the pastor of which is the Rev. Mr. Black, who was a fellow-passenger on the boat from Scottsburg. He seemed to be a real blockhead.

We transferred here to another steamboat which took us out of the bay into the broad expanse of the Pacific Ocean. I hail thee, mighty Pacific, for the very first time! The word "pacific" seems out of place here, however, for the mighty waves come crashing in upon the rocky shoreline with a roar that can be heard many miles away. The thunder of the mighty breakers makes conversation along the shore utterly impossible. Our boat drew alongside a promontory, but because of shallow water it could not bring us to land; so we transferred to a much smaller boat and this brought us to dockside, where a stagecoach awaited us.

And now came an unparalleled stagecoach ride on the hard, smooth sand of the ocean beach just beyond the water's edge. At ebb tide the ocean beach makes as fine a road as one can imagine. The wheels of the stage are about six inches wide and therefore do not sink into the moist, smooth sand. And what a glorious ocean scene. Here and there along the route the sea breaks over nearby rocks and throws a blanket of misty spray over the wayfarer. Far out on the horizon the white sails of a ship are silhouetted against the sky. Great flocks of gulls, cranes, and herons flap, flutter, and stalk along the water's edge looking for food. Here and there a seal sloshes his way through the shallow tide. To the east, long stretches of sand dunes reach out to meet the dense green pine forests.

Presently we left the road along the beach and turned inland across the sand prairie to Coos Bay. Here we entered a rowboat and were taken about a mile and a half across the bay to Empire, a little settlement with a big sawmill. Here we spent the night in a good hotel.

November 20. We reached Marshfield this forenoon. This is a small town with a population of about eight hundred. It is certainly not a very beautiful place, but it has a good harbor. There are a good many Finnish Swedes who have settled here and in the vicinity of Coos Bay. The total for this area is said to be between six and seven hundred. The earliest settlements were made fourteen or fifteen years ago. The people in these parts are hard-working, industrious folk who will doubtless make good use of their opportunities out here. Religiously, this is the most promising field I have yet encountered on my western expedition.

November 22. On this Sunday it has rained intermittently. This has, nevertheless, been a great festive day in Marshfield. This morning we celebrated Holy Communion. I preached the preparatory sermon while Carlson delivered the gospel sermon for the day. There was a good attendance. This afternoon at two o'clock we held the festive dedication service for the new church building in Marshfield. First there was an English service at which I preached on the text Luke 13:18-21. Thereupon Carlson delivered the dedicatory address, and this was followed by the rite of dedication which I conducted. An offering of forty-five dollars was received for the benefit of the congregation. In the evening we installed the new pastor, G. M. Ryden. I preached the sermon and conducted the rite of installation. The congregation was very attentive and seemed to be impressed by what they witnessed.

177

It rained hard during the evening and on into the night. I was very tired after the exertions of the day. We were housed in the home of Mr. and Mrs. Lund, who live near the church. They are fine people.

November 26. Because of the constant downpour of rain no boats have been running, so we have been unable to leave Marshfield. We have stayed here and enjoyed the hospitality of these friends. Today, however, we received word that the boats are again moving, so we bade our kind friends in Marshfield goodbye and started back toward Empire. Just as we were leaving a couple of friends came to me and handed me $11.25, which the people had collected to pay for the expenses of my journey. God bless them. When we arrived in Empire we boarded a boat bound for San Francisco. The fare was $7.50, which was the half-fare clergy rate.

The weather cleared, and about noon our boat left the harbor. As we came out on the open sea the wind began to blow and the waves tossed our boat like a leaf.

We bravely sat down at the dining table for our noon meal, but before I had taken many bites I was compelled to hurry to the rail to feed the fish. We crept into our bunks and stayed there almost the entire time. It took us sixty-two hours, three nights and two and a half days, to reach Frisco. Although land was visible most of the way, the rough seas made the trip a miserable experience.

November 29. We arrived in Frisco about two o'clock in the morning but stayed in our bunks on board ship until daylight. We hired a cab, which took us to the home of the local Swedish pastor, John Telleen. There we bathed and breakfasted and then received our instructions. I was to stay in Frisco and preach at both the forenoon and evening services, while the Rev. Mr. Carlson was to go to San Jose and conduct services there.

The Swedish Lutheran church here is an attractive and stately edifice with excellent appointments. The music at the services was good, but the attendance was somewhat small. It was a pleasant experience to proclaim the Word of God for these my countrymen. There are many who are genuine Christians. There is great cause for rejoicing over the progress which our beloved Lutheran church has been making in San Francisco. The diligent labors of the Rev. Mr. Telleen have been very fruitful. It would be well if he could stay here for a longer period. He has a call to our congregation in Rockford, Illinois, but has not yet decided whether or not to accept it.

November 30. I awakened in good health and good spirits this morning. Praise God! The weather is like summertime. Today we toured the city. From the outlying bluffs one can get a good view of the whole surrounding area. The streetcars in San Francisco are excellent and render good service to the people. The cable cars are particularly noteworthy and famous, taking passengers with ease up and down the steep hills in town. From Telegraph Hill the view of the bay is magnificent. Oakland and several other cities can be seen across the bay.

In the afternoon Carlson and Telleen returned to the city and Brother Carlson boasted that San Jose was the most charming city he had ever seen.

December 1. This forenoon we had a series of conferences to plan and arrange for the work here in view of Telleen's decision to move away from here. The education of his children and the health of his wife are valid reasons for him to leave. One must, of course, take care of one's own family, but it will be difficult to secure a successor for Brother Telleen. He has even suggested that I accept a call from this congregation. This is impossible since my health would not permit me to undertake this strenuous labor. I could perhaps manage to care for the congregation for a limited time.

In the afternoon we visited Woodward's Gardens, an unusually attractive park with an interesting zoo. By evening I was worn out.

December 4. Another beautiful day. I left San Francisco at

about eleven o'clock this morning, bound for San Jose. My ticket cost $1.75. Arrived in San Jose at noon. I ate lunch in the Union House Restaurant, operated by a Swede named Swensson who came originally from Engelholm, Sweden. I looked up a certain widow, Mrs. Allen, who resides on the east side of the city. She was born in Finland, is rich, and has a very attractive home. I rented lodging from her. Several members of her family reside with her, and they all speak Finnish, Swedish, and English. I think I shall like it here.

December 6, Second Sunday in Advent. I preached and conducted services in the forenoon as well as this evening. There was an attendance of twenty people. The building which our Swedish congregation is erecting is not yet finished and is only partially enclosed. It is attractively situated.

December 10. I have been ill since last Sunday and have kept to my room, so that I am just as unacquainted with the people of this congregation here as I was upon my arrival.

Yesterday I received a letter from the Mission Board of the synod inviting me to become the superintendent of our missionary work on the west coast. What shall I answer? Perhaps I can accept this task until the forthcoming synodical convention next spring.

December 13, Third Sunday in Advent. The weather is clear and bright. I preached at our services this morning, which were held at 10:30. There were about fifteen persons present. This is very discouraging, but one must not give up hope. The Norwegian pastor, a member of the Norwegian Synod, by the name of Didriksen, was in town today. Since our work is beginning to prosper, he visits this community more frequently. He is said to associate with lodge people and saloon keepers. This evening I preached on the subject of man's fall into sin and his great need for a Savior. There were about fifty people in attendance.

December 14. Today I have felt weak and ill. Have spent

most of the day writing letters and catching up on all my correspondence. I have accepted the invitation to become, for the time being, the superintendent of our missionary work on the west coast.

The financial situation involving the local congregation as well as the Rev. Mr. Telleen, and the fact that the lumber bill for the new building is far past due, made it necessary for me to ask Telleen to come to San Jose and get the matter cleared up.

December 16. Telleen has succeeded in arranging a new loan at the bank for one thousand dollars. Thus, the vacant lots owned by the congregation will not need to be sold. The total debt amounts to a little more than three thousand dollars. If there were genuine church unity and interest in this congregation it would be relatively easy to liquidate this debt. Telleen left for home about noon today but intends to return again next week to straighten out the affairs of this congregation further. He promised to find us an organist for our forthcoming Christmas services. That will be well, for if I am compelled to lead the singing as well as preach I will surely collapse. He told me that the congregation in San Francisco wants to call me as his successor there.

December 22. I am not feeling well these days, although I have tried to doctor myself. I am depressed. My circumstances here are ambiguous. Why am I here? Where shall I turn? Jealousy, distrust, and trouble surround me. Back home in Minnesota the conference authorities plan for my destruction. Out here I do not really feel at home, and my health is so poor that I am unable to labor as I ought and as the circumstances demand.

This afternoon Telleen paid me a visit and reported that he had secured an organist for us from San Francisco. He has also succeeded in straightening out the business affairs of the congregation by getting another loan from the bank. I pray that this indebtedness may be liquidated before it overwhelms the congregation.

December 24, Christmas Eve. A strange and wonderful Christmas Eve, since it is the first green Christmas I have ever celebrated in all my life. My health is somewhat better. I have been preparing for the early Matins service in the morning. This evening was spent in the traditional way here in the home, and I presented Christmas presents to the various members of the family, for which they seemed genuinely grateful. There was no Christmas present for me. How I long for my own family, my dear wife and children, my home, and my beloved congregation. I spent the latter part of the evening alone in my room recalling past Christmases. Outside the rain poured, and though the weather was not cold there was a real chill in my room. Tonight my thoughts are with my loved ones, and I know they pray for me even as I pray for them. O Lord, grant that we may again be reunited as a family. Blessed Jesus, thou didst come to our sinful world; come even now to my heart and fill me with childlike faith and love to thee. Help me on the morrow to proclaim thy truth to thy glory. Amen.

December 25. Christmas! Holy and joyous Christmastide! I bid thee welcome. Thou hast a strange power over these human hearts. I arose this morning at 3 A.M. I had coffee in bed. The heavens are clear and star-lit. By 4 A.M. we were at the church. The decorations in the church were excellent and tasteful. I conducted the full liturgical service for morning worship. I preached about the song of the angels. There were about a hundred people present.

This evening we had our Sunday school program in the church. Two beautiful Christmas trees laden with tinsel and decorations were placed in the chancel. We sang the old familiar Christmas songs. I gave a talk about Christmas and the children. Two small girls gave recitations in English, and the Sunday school sang two Swedish Christmas carols. The entire program was edifying and well done. There were again about a hundred people present.

December 27, First Sunday after Christmas. Today I opened

the service with three people present and no organist. A few late-comers swelled the congregation to a final total of ten. The reason so few came out for worship was that the Swedish folk in town had been out dancing last night until almost dawn and therefore found it impossible to come out for services. This kind of response is exceedingly discouraging for a missionary, but what can a man do? One cannot despair but must continue patiently to invite, instruct, and urge, and hope that in his own good time the Lord will win a few souls. It seems that spiritual concern is almost extinct here. Many of these people never came into contact with a vital Christianity back home in Sweden, and since coming to this country they have become even more indifferent to religion and the church. May the Lord have mercy upon them and awaken them while there is still time.

December 31. This is the last day of the year 1885. Oh, how I miss my dear family and long for them! May the Lord help, bless, and keep them all! Tonight at midnight a tremendous racket broke out all over town as the people welcomed in the new year with shooting and noise of all kinds.

Yesterday we had a slight earthquake here. The houses rocked slightly. In San Francisco the tremor was much more severe and frightened people out of their houses and homes.

January 1, 1886. Welcome, thou New Year of the Lord! This is a beautiful day. I conducted morning worship at the church and preached to a very small congregation.

January 3, Sunday after New Year. The old year is gone but the old sins remain. No sin is greater than the despising of God's Word. Today at the service of worship there were about fifteen people present. I met a widow by the name of Anna L. Tell who lives in Santa Clara, about three miles from here. She seems to be a pious and sincere Christian. How encouraging it is to meet a true Christian in the midst of the prevailing indifference.

I have made a change in the hour of worship. I announced that the hour for service next Sunday will be 2:30 in the afternoon. We shall see if this is a more convenient hour for the people to attend church. Since Christmas I have felt so ill and weak that I have been unable to preach more than once each Sunday.

January 5. This is an unusually beautiful day—and they call this winter! Nevertheless, this is a wonderful climate. I took a trip to Santa Clara today by streetcar and called on Widow Tell. While she is a concerned Christian, her two daughters and one son-in-law, who live with her, show no interest whatever in religion or church.

January 10, First Sunday after Epiphany. We had services in church today. I preached to sixteen people. It seems as if the Swedish people in this community have determined not to attend the Swedish Lutheran church here. They very likely are afraid of the financial obligation of church membership, and besides they undoubtedly do not like the kind of Christianity that is preached here. The Norwegian preacher, Didriksen, is most likely doing what he can to awaken antagonism against us. He is a friend to lodge members and saloon keepers.

January 17, Second Sunday after Epiphany. Today we had morning worship with celebration of the Lord's Supper. The text for my preparatory sermon was I John 1:8-9. There were only five people who came to the Lord's table. I hope they were sincere and penitent souls. I bade the congregation farewell and announced that the Rev. F. O. Linder, the new pastor, would be here for services next Sunday. My fervent prayer is that this dear brother will be the Lord's instrument to draw many into the kingdom. I believe he will get along well here, since he is a gifted man, patient, industrious, and even musical.

January 18. I have settled my accounts with Mrs. Allen, who charged me thirty dollars for room and board for six weeks. I have had excellent quarters here in the Allen home. May the Lord bless her and comfort her in her anxiety over her shiftless son Alex-

184

ander. I bade them all a hearty farewell. Alexander went with me to the depot, where I caught the train for San Francisco.

I arrived in Frisco about 2:30 in the afternoon and went directly to the home of the Rev. Mr. Telleen, where I met Pastor and Mrs. Linder and also Pastor Peter Carlson, who had just arrived from Sacramento. We were now four Lutheran pastors gathered under one roof, and we had a truly glorious and edifying fellowship as we talked about many things and made plans about the missionary work on the west coast.

In the evening an informal service was held in the undercroft of the church, with Carlson delivering the sermon. There were not many present.

January 19. It is raining steadily today. We continue our conversations and our planning concerning church work and religious matters for this area. We had evening services at which I preached on the text Luke 12:32. It is strange, but it seems that my health and well-being are better here in San Francisco than in San Jose.

January 20. Today is a very stormy and rainy day. Telegraph lines, railroads, ships, and houses have suffered wind and water damage. This afternoon, during a lull in the storm, Telleen and I traveled to San Rafael, about twenty-five miles north of Frisco, where a number of Swedish settlers reside. We first took a ferry, then boarded a train which took us through three tunnels, over several small bays, and across some valleys. At several places along the way the water came up over the tracks. It seemed as if we would never get through, but we finally made it to San Rafael. We found lodging with a Norwegian by the name of Hansen, who is married to a Swedish woman. We were able to gather about a dozen people in the Hansen home for a devotional service this evening. I gave a brief meditation on a portion of Matthew 16. Telleen also gave a brief message.

January 21. Telleen returned home today, but I remained here in San Rafael. I conducted a catechetical class with two daughters of a widow by the name of Nelson who came here three years ago from New Bedford, Massachusetts. The girls did very well and are well-behaved children. May God protect and nurture them for his kingdom!

At 11:30 A.M. I took the train back to San Francisco, where I arrived just after the noon hour. I was informed that the Rev. Mr. Linder left earlier today for his new field in San Jose. Carlson was also here when I arrived but left during the afternoon for Sacramento. This evening we had an informal devotional service at church. Telleen preached the sermon.

January 27. It has been raining almost continuously for the past several days, and I have therefore been unable to make any missionary trips. The railroads are washed out in many places, and at others the tracks are under several feet of water. Here in San Francisco, however, we have had devotional services every evening, at a number of which I have preached. The other day I received one hundred and fifty dollars as salary. I sent twenty-five dollars home to my wife. I have received reports from Pastors Carlson, Ryden, and Linder. They labor in their respective fields with diligence. I had word also from the Rev. Mr. Anderson in Tacoma. He, too, is busy. O Lord, bless these brethren, give them power, wisdom, and courage!

January 29. The Rev. Mr. Telleen and I went to Oakland, where I consulted Dr. Liljencrantz concerning my health. He suggested that I spend a few days at the sulfur baths in Paraiso Springs in Monterey County. We also visited Berkeley and Alcatraz. A number of Swedish families have settled in this area.

February 1. Today I bade farewell to Brother Telleen and traveled to Saguel, in Santa Cruz County. The fare was $3.50. I rented a room at Camp Capitola on the shore of Santa Cruz Bay. This is a summer vacation resort, and many cottages are now empty. The hotel rate here is reasonable. I paid only one dollar for a night's lodging.

February 2. This morning I went to the village of Saguel, about a mile north of the depot. From there I went another mile north of the village to find a Swedish settler named Oliver. He has a farm of one hundred and sixty acres with excellent buildings and no indebtedness. Mr. Oliver was not at home but I spoke to his wife and family. Mrs. Oliver was confirmed in Sweden but has joined the Congregational church in Saguel. Mr. Oliver is a lodge member and has no interest in the church. There are six other Swedish families scattered around this area, several of whom have joined the Congregational church. The prospects for a Lutheran mission here are very dim and unpromising.

In spite of the discouraging outlook I must visit Santa Cruz inasmuch as I am so near. About three o'clock in the afternoon I went to Santa Cruz, which I found to be a very attractive little city lying in an oval valley of the bay.

February 3. I left Santa Cruz about noon and went to Monterey, about forty miles away. The fare was two dollars. Monterey is an old Mexican town, and it looks the part. More than half of the people are Mexicans and speak Spanish. The streets are ill kept and crooked and run in all directions. There are numerous adobe houses and old ruins. Some of the old adobe ruins look spooky. On the east side of town there is an old Catholic church situated by the side of a waterfall, further evidence of the ingenuity with which the Roman church so often chooses its church sites.

February 4. This is a beautiful day, but I do not feel well. I caught a cold in Santa Cruz. I left Monterey at one o'clock this afternoon, bound for Soledad. We crossed the Saline River and took a stagecoach to Paraiso Springs. It was pitch dark when we arrived in Paraiso Springs. I have already taken a drink of the sulphur water, which makes my throat feel somewhat better.

February 7, Fifth Sunday after Epiphany. I slept well last night; awoke early but went back to sleep again. When I awoke the second time the sun was shining brightly and the birds were singing merrily. Today shall be a day of real rest for me, the first I have had since I left home. I have been drinking the sulphur water and have bathed in the medicinal water, relaxing, resting, and just dreaming the hours away. This salubrious climate is conducive to such a state of mind. It is about 80 degrees in the shade. The peach trees are in full bloom, and many varieties of colorful wild flowers bloom in luxuriant abundance.

I have read several sections of my New Testament and have enjoyed a quiet fellowship with my Lord. Thanks be to God for this good day! It has surely been a wonderful blessing to me.

February 11. I slept well last night. The weather is beautiful, praise God for his goodness. I arose at sunup and drank some mineral water. Had my breakfast and then paid my bill of fourteen dollars for the past week. At nine o'clock this forenoon I took the stage from Paraiso Springs. I am sure that my stay there has improved my health. I did not meet any spiritually minded people at Paraiso Springs, although there are said to be several Swedish families scattered throughout the surrounding area. I arrived back in San Francisco a little after six o'clock in the evening. I found the Telleen family in good health and the usual circumstances. I will remain here over Sunday.

February 15. I left San Francisco at two o'clock this afternoon for Santa Rosa in Sanama County, about fifty miles away. At Santa Rosa we are at a higher elevation than San Francisco. A sparse growth of white oak spreads across this section, and the city of Santa Rosa is attractively situated. I secured a room at the Grand Hotel. I have been told that there are a few Swedish families in and around the town, but I have not yet met them.

February 16. This morning at about 10:30 A.M. I took the train from Santa Rosa to Cloverdale. The fare was $1.75. I arrived in Cloverdale about noon and ate lunch there. In Cloverdale I took the stage to Ukiah, the county seat of Mendocino County, some thirty-two miles distant. The road follows the Russian River through a picturesque but wild and desolate countryside. We arrived in Ukiah about six o'clock in the evening, thoroughly shaken up by the rough ride. I secured a room at the Palace Hotel which seems to be a respectable, clean place.

February 17. I awakened early this morning to a beautiful day. After breakfast I walked around town and struck up conversations with several people regarding this part of the country. The major occupation in this region is sheep raising with some fruit and vegetable farming. There are no prospects for our church here. I had hoped to proceed to Anderson Valley, where I am told there are a few Swedish settlers, but I have discovered that the stage line does not go to Anderson Valley and therefore I shall return to Cloverdale and from there go on to San Francisco.

February 22. I bade farewell this day to my friends in San Francisco and took a train to Marysville, in Yuba County. I stayed overnight in the Western Hotel in Marysville.

February 23. I took a stage to Yuba City, the county seat of Sutter County. Here in Yuba City I have rented a room from a Mr. Phipps, who introduced me to a Swedish family by the name of Pihl. This family came originally from Norrköping in Sweden and has been here several years. The Pihls operate a rooming house and saloon. They told me that a number of Swedish farmers have settled near Sutter Station in Sutter County.

February 24. I hired a rig to take me from Yuba City to Sutter Station, a distance of about thirteen miles. The cost was six dollars. The road runs along the Feather River. Sutter County is a level area located between the Feather and the Sacramento rivers, which are often flooded during the rainy season. There is an old abandoned railroad grade which runs through this section from Yuba City to Knight's Landing, along which the Sutter Station settlement is located. It is here that I found the Swedish settlers. There are about six families, and the leaders are John Sutherland and Peter Olson. The Swedish population perhaps totals about forty souls, including children. Some of these settlers have been here for sixteen years. Several families own as much as a half section of land, but they are not as prosperous as they might be since their land is so often flooded and their crops destroyed.

March 2. I have held services and preached five times, and have had a number of catechetical sessions with the children of Sutter Station. The people here are religiously inclined, but they have become somewhat infected with the notions of the Methodists and Mission Covenanters.[4] If these people can be properly taken care of, we could very likely establish a Lutheran congregation here. In general these settlers are a sturdy, dependable people. They have given me a gift of twelve dollars. I have arranged to leave the settlement tomorrow.

March 13. The wind has been blowing hard all day here in San Francisco. The sand has drifted like snow across the streets. My eyes have been giving me a good deal of trouble, so that I feared that I was losing the sight in my right eye. Therefore this afternoon I went to an eye doctor by the name of Dr. C. Muller, who gave me an eye examination. The examination took a long time, and when it was over the doctor said I had "very bad eyes" and "almost no eyes at all." He finally found some glasses which helped my vision both far and near, but at a cost of thirty dollars. I had no alternative but to pay the price he asked or go around like a blind man, so I took the glasses. Dr. Muller has the reputation of being a competent physician.

March 14. After a brief prayer service with my dear friends the Telleens, I bade them farewell and at ten o'clock this morning boarded a steamship, "State of California," headed for Astoria, Oregon. O Lord, I thank thee for the experiences thou hast brought to me here in California.

---

[4] "Mission Covenanters" refers to followers of the Swedish revivalist, Peter Paul Waldenstrom (1838-1917). They formed the Swedish Evangelical Mission Covenant Church in America in 1885.

In many respects California is a remarkable and wonderful section of our country, but it has its dark and unattractive sides also. In general, the arable land is much too expensive. Nevertheless, I predict that many more of our Swedish countrymen will find their way out here in the future.

The ticket to Astoria cost fifteen dollars. It was most pleasant to cruise through the calm waters of San Francisco Bay under a bright and warm sun. But as soon as we came out on the Pacific Ocean our boat began to pitch and rock, and it was not long before I was thoroughly seasick and had to crawl into my bunk. We did not encounter stormy weather, but the sea was far from calm.

March 16. We arrived in Astoria this morning between nine and ten o'clock. It was snowing when we landed, and the sight of falling snow was something new after our stay in California. I took a streetcar to the home of Mr. Gust Holmes, where I was given a hearty welcome by Mrs. Holmes. Mr. Holmes is a fisherman and at present is on a fishing voyage and will not return for some time.

March 21. The past several days have been wet and cold. People here must splash around like ducks. There are a number of Swedish families residing here in Astoria, most of whom have no interest in church or religion. It is most unfortunate that we do not have a pastor here. The Norwegians and Danes hold their services in our Swedish church. The bickering and disagreements between the Norwegains and Danes serve no purpose except to confuse the people and alienate the community.

I have held several services here. Last Friday evening I conducted a Lenten service in our church with an encouraging number of people attending.

Today, which is the Second Sunday in Lent, I held services and preached at both the forenoon and evening meetings. This afternoon I went to a farmer's home and baptized two infants of

Swedish families. The attendance at the services of worship has been encouraging.

March 22. It continues to rain almost constantly. Today I had my noon meal with Mr. August Olson, the janitor and caretaker of our church property here in Astoria. He is a former seaman and comes originally from Kälmar, Sweden. I settled my account with Mrs. Holmes and bade her farewell, then boarded the steamship "R. R. Thompson" this evening. I am spending the night on board ship because we leave port early in the morning bound for Portland.

March 23. Rain mixed with hail fell all night. Between Astoria and Portland there is not much to see. The scenery consists mostly of high bluffs overgrown with dense pine forests. We passed several fishing fleets along the route. We arrived in Portland at three o'clock this afternoon. The Rev. Mr. Skans was at the dock to meet me, and I went home with him.

March 31. After several days of dry, warm weather it has now begun to rain here in Portland. We have conducted several services and devotional meetings during our stay here. I have now decided to travel to Moscow, Idaho, and stay there for a couple of weeks. May the Lord bless this journey!

April 1. This day I left Portland about 3:30 P.M. The fare to Moscow, Idaho, is $19.55. The train is very crowded. I must get some rest even though I must sit up the entire way to Moscow.

April 2. The rain continues to pour. Our train moves very slowly and cautiously. The railroad follows the Palouse River, and we have passed through the towns of Endicott, Colfax, and Poulman. Here and there along the tracks are large storage bins for grain. A little after five o'clock this afternoon we arrived in Moscow. The surrounding countryside is hilly, but it seems suitable for raising wheat. Some five miles northwest of town there is a high mountain range, and another lower range is visible toward the southeast. I looked up a certain Mr. Ramstedt, who is a tenant of the Rev. Peter Carlson, and was heartily welcomed, even though my coming was entirely unexpected.[5]

April 4, Fourth Sunday in Lent. We have hired the Presbyterian church in Moscow for our services. This morning I preached on the text for the day, John 6. There were about thirty people present and they all seemed very attentive. It is good to speak to people who genuinely hunger for God's Word.

April 5. This is a chilly, blustery day. One of the members of the congregation here in Moscow, Mr. Olof Olson, drove me around the countryside today so that I could inspect our missionary prospects here.

April 6. I spent the night in the little home of Olof Olson. Like practically everyone else out here, the Olsons are living the life of pioneers; they are well acquainted with poverty and deprivation, but with patience and diligent labor they will undoubtedly succeed eventually.

Mr. Olson again drove me around the surrounding area, particularly west of Moscow to a section called Paradise Valley. On the way we passed through a place called Hog Heaven. Our route took us up through some high bluffs from which we had an excellent view of the valley below. Far to the northwest we could see the Blue Mountains, and to the northeast the Bitter Root range with Mt. Idaho peak clearly visible. After driving around for a while, the trail petered out and we had to guess our way toward the Swedish settlement of Cordelia, which was said to be located somewhere in the region. We finally came to the Cordelia Swedish Lutheran church, which is surely the smallest church building in the entire Augustana Synod. We found the farmhouse of Peter Anderson, one of the leaders of the community, and here we were heartily welcomed.

---

[5] Peter Carlson had purchased a farm near Moscow, Idaho, and his family made their home there while Carlson traveled throughout his widespread mission field in the Pacific northwest.

April 9. While Mr. Olson returned to Moscow, I have remained in Cordelia in order to inspect the territory during the last few days. This evening I conducted a Lenten devotional service in the little church. There was a good attendance. I was invited for dinner this noon to the home of Andrew Olson, who formerly resided in Vasa, Minnesota. He and his family seem to be getting along tolerably well, although they live like pioneers on the frontier. They have two quarters of land, a few cattle, and some hogs. Andrew Olson's brother also owns a farm nearby, but he rents out the land to a tenant while he has a job in Colton, Oregon.

April 10. I had a good night's sleep. Praise God for continued health and strength to soul and body! As I trudge to and fro among these Swedish settlers and see how poor many of them are, how simple and downright uncomfortable many of the homes are, and under what primitive conditions pioneers must exist, I am reminded of the rugged times I spent in Minnesota just a few years ago. I doubt that I have the strength and stamina to endure such trials now. I know that the Rev. Peter Carlson has endured incredible deprivations since coming out here to carry on the mission of the church. I hope he can find a somewhat less demanding field now that he is getting older. It is nearly impossible to interpret for people in the East what life on the western frontier is really like.

April 11, Fifth Sunday in Lent. I conducted divine worship and preached in the little church this forenoon. The attendance was encouraging. Olof Olson from Moscow came for me with his buckboard and brought me back to Moscow this afternoon. We took the northern route, which is much less precipitous than the southern route which we took coming out. It was a moving and emotional experience to say farewell to the dear Swedish people in the Cordelia settlement.

April 12. I am staying in the home of Gustaf Johnson, a member of the Moscow congregation. Mr. Johnson was one of the very first Swedes to settle in this vicinity. He came here about five years ago from St. James, Minnesota. He has a tolerably good house and a large family of seven children, five girls and two boys. He is a carpenter and can earn as high as three dollars a day. He tells me that a good plasterer can make up to five dollars a day, because it is so difficult to find this kind of craftsman out here. Out here one has to pay five dollars a barrel for plaster. It is no wonder that there are only two houses in the whole town which have plastered walls. It costs five dollars to have a team of horses shod. The cost of farm machinery and implements is at least double what it is back East. There is no hardwood out here to make wagons of, and labor costs are much greater.

Mr. Johnson tells me that the climate is very temperate all year long, neither too hot nor too cold. It seems to me that this would be a good place for Swedish people to settle. The worst criticism I have heard is that the land is somewhat hilly and hard to cultivate, although the soil is rich and productive. The average yield of wheat is about thirty to forty bushels to the acre; flax-seed, about twenty bushels per acre; potatoes, from one hundred to one hundred and fifty bushels per acre; and corn, from fifty to sixty bushels per acre.

April 15. I left Moscow yesterday by train, bound for Alkali, Idaho, where I arrived at 1:25 in the morning. I was met at the depot by Mr. J. E. Peterson, who lives in Alkali. I have become acquainted with two young Swedish laborers here, both of whom work as section hands on the railroad. They are Fred Hanson and John Johnson. They both live in the station house. Alkali is a small town with fairly good buildings but with altogether too many saloons. The town has only one decent street. Not many Swedish people live here.

April 16. After hiring a rig and persuading John Johnson to accompany me as my driver, I left Alkali this morning about 6:30. We followed a ravine for some twelve miles southeast. We then came to a plateau known as Shuttle Flat. Here there was a settlement of well-built homes. After traveling another twenty miles we stopped for lunch. We begged some water for our coffee from a farmer and then, driving down into a ravine, we built a fire and cooked our coffee and beans. Johnson is a masterful cook and served up a tasty meal. As we continued our journey in the afternoon the wind began to blow and a flurry of snow sent the temperature down. We finally reached a small shanty with a slanting roof. This was the home of a Swedish settler by the name of Carl Anderson. Here we found lodging for the night.

April 18, Palm Sunday. Today I held festive services in the shanty home of Carl Anderson. I administered Holy Communion to twenty Swedish settlers who are Anderson's neighbors. In the afternoon I baptized several children and preached a sermon on Christ's passion. The people have requested another service to be held tomorrow at ten o'clock in the forenoon in the home of another settler, Mr. Jonas Johnson. There is also talk about organizing a congregation at that service.

April 19. On this Monday after Palm Sunday we assembled in the modest home of Jonas Johnson, who came out here several years ago from Lindsborg, Kansas. I conducted a regular morning worship service and preached on the text for Good Friday. After the service, while the women were busy preparing dinner for the assembly, we men went outside and sat down on a pile of fence posts and constituted ourselves a quorum for the purpose of organizing a Swedish Lutheran congregation. I opened the meeting with prayer, and I was then elected to preside at the meeting. After some discussion it was resolved to establish a congregation under the name of the Swedish Evangelical Lutheran Congregation of Walby, Morrow County, Oregon. It was also resolved to petition for membership in the Augustana Lutheran Synod. The total communicant membership inscribed on the charter roll is seventeen. It was also recommended that a pastoral visit be made to the congregation in the fall when the men return from the annual sheep-shearing expedition up in the hill country. If I cannot return to these people, Pastor Peter Carlson will most likely make the visit.

This settlement could become an important center for our church work if more of our Swedish countrymen would find their way to this place in the near future. The land is plentiful and cheap; there is room for several hundred families. Although it is forty or fifty miles to the nearest railroad, the roads are fairly good with no hazardous precipices. Abundant sources of wood may be had in the Blue Mountains, about twenty miles distant. The settlers are permitted to take from government land all the wood they need. The climate is salubrious, and the winters are mild with very moderate snowfall. Both grain and fruit, together with practically all kinds of vegetables, can be produced here. Most of the free land has already been claimed by homesteaders. The government has given away other sections of land to the Northern Pacific Railroad. Many settlers have purchased their holdings from the railroad. But if the government should ever reclaim the railroad holdings, a very great deal of land would then be made available as homesteads. Many farmers are digging their own wells and are finding good, sweet water at a depth of only fifteen or twenty feet.

After the meeting was concluded I accompanied Mr. N. M. Peterson and his family to their home. I shall stay here another day or two to look over the field more thoroughly.

April 21. Today John Johnson and I left Walby and returned to Alkali. We arrived here about six o'clock this evening. I am staying here in the railroad section house with my generous host, John Johnson. The train will stop here at two o'clock in the morning, and I will take it to Portland.

April 22. I arrived in Portland this forenoon at ten o'clock. The Rev. Mr. Skans met me at the depot and took me to his home, which is in the undercroft of the church. The Rev. Mr. Lindh from

La Conner, Washington, also arrived here today, en route to Nehalem for a pastoral visit. He preached the sermon at the devotional service this evening. I have had a splitting headache all day.

April 23, Good Friday. I feel somewhat better but am worn out from my long trip. This evening I preached in a country schoolhouse for thirty or forty people.

April 25, Easter Sunday. Hail thou risen and living Lord, Jesus Christ! The weather today is perfect; all nature joins with the Christian church in the joy of Easter. At the festive Easter service this forenoon I preached about the great theme of Christ's resurrection and his victory over death. The church was well-filled. At the service this evening the attendance was even better, and again it was my privilege to proclaim the great message of Easter to our people.

April 27. The Rev. Mr. Lindh returned today from his visit in Nehalem. He reports that there are some twenty to twenty-five Swedish families living in and around Nehalem and that a Swedish Lutheran congregation ought to be established there. It is somewhat difficult to reach Nehalem, since one must walk many miles over a mountain pass to reach the place.

This evening I spoke to a meeting of young people of the Portland congregation. My subject was "The Imperatives for a Successful Young People's Society."

April 28. Today I left Portland and accompanied Lindh to his home in La Conner. We took a boat to Vancouver and from there drove in a wagon ten or twelve miles into the forest. Here the settlers have accomplished unbelievable work. Clearings in the dense forest, with thousands of tree stumps and great piles of slashings, are encountered on every hand. Here the people live and eke out a livelihood, keeping a cow or two, some chickens, and perhaps a few hogs.

The La Conner community is a mixture of several nationalities. Finns, Swedes, Americans, Germans, a few Danes, Frenchmen, and others live together and share the hardships and triumphs of pioneer life. Here are some very sturdy, dependable people who make good church members. Lindh has labored diligently here, and his wife is a great help to him.

There is no free government land in this area. Virgin land can be purchased for seven or eight dollars an acre higher up toward the mountains.

April 29. This afternoon at two o'clock I held a devotional service in a country schoolhouse for the Swedish settlers in the neighborhood. This evening I preached in English to the entire community, and the people seemed grateful to hear God's Word. One man came up to me after the service and said, "You are a brother of mine; I can tell by the way you talk."

April 30. Today I returned to Portland, where we shall hold a district meeting for our pastors. I reached Portland about six o'clock this evening.

May 3. Today the assembled pastors met for consultation about our missionary work here in the West. I was chosen to be the presiding officer for the meeting, with the Rev. Mr. Telleen as vice-president, the Rev. G. A. Anderson as secretary, and the Rev. J. W. Skans as treasurer. We canvassed the entire mission field in our discussion, and it was reported that the field on the West coast now comprises seventeen congregations with ten church buildings and two parsonages.

May 4. The meeting of missionary pastors continued today. Sermons were given by Pastors Telleen, Ryden, and myself. It was a blessed time of fellowship. At the conclusion of our session we bade one another an affectionate farewell.

May 5. Today the missionary pastors all returned to their respective homes. At 3:30 this afternoon I boarded the train for St. Paul, Minnesota. My ticket cost thirty-five dollars. It was a most moving experience to part company with these dear brethren with whom I have had such an enriching fellowship during these past months.

May 6. We reached Wallula Junction last night about 3 A.M. Here I was able to secure a bed in an immigrant sleeping car. For one dollar I rented a mattress filled with shavings, and with my overcoat as a pillow I tried to get some sleep.

May 9. When I awoke this morning our train was near Wadena, Minnesota. We arrived in St. Paul about 12:30 this noon. My son, Theodore, was at the station to meet me, and we had our midday meal together. I took the train to Red Wing, where my son Leonard, in company with my neighbor Solomon Nelson, met me and drove me home to Vasa, where with greatest joy and gratitude I was reunited with my dear wife and family. Praised be the Lord, who has protected and kept me and my loved ones during this long and eventful missionary journey!

INDEX

INDEX

Abrahamson, Olof, 53
American Indian, 89f.
American West, 10f.
Andersen, Paul, 59, 59n, 146
Anderson, Abram, 71
Anderson, Carl, 148
Anderson, C. J., 139
Anderson, G. A., 165, 174, 186, 199
Anderson, Jöns Per, 55, 66, 69-71
Anderson, Jon, 133
Anderson, Karin, 56
Anderson, P. M., 133
Andreen, A., 140, 143, 144, 146, 154, 155
Andreen, O. C. T., 154
Andover, Illinois, 4, 6, 14, 49ff., 61, 63, 65, 67, 70, 132, 139
Anfinson, Ole, 143, 144
Attica, Indiana, 23, 35
Augsburg Confession, 118n, 142, 146
Augustana, 37, 164
Augustana Lutheran Synod, 7, 9, 10n, 16, 17, 21, 22, 23, 25, 26, 29, 31, 36, 37, 156n

Augustana Pension and Aid Fund, 22

Bengston, Olaus, 71
Berglof, Stephen, 65
Berlin, Illinois, 20
Bergenlund, B. G., 146, 147, 154
Bethel Ship, 55, 124
Bishop Hill, Illinois, 65, 133, 133n, 135
Bonneville, Ore., 160
Buffalo Lutheran Synod, 125, 125n
Burlington, Iowa, 73

Cannon Falls, Minnesota, 151, 155
Capital University, 7, 14, 32, 75n, 78f., 89, 99n, 115, 140
Carlson, Peter, 26, 33, 149, 174, 175, 177, 178, 179, 185, 186, 194, 197
Carlsson, Erland, 123, 123n, 127, 128, 131, 135, 136, 139, 142, 145, 146, 147, 154, 193n
Carver, Minnesota, 34

Carnival, 104f.
Cascade Lake, Ore., 160
Cavallin, John O., 156
Cedarstam, P. A., 26, 142, 145, 147, 149, 154, 155, 168
Cervin, A. R., 154
Chicago Conference, 143, 144, see also United Scandinavian Conference
Chisago Lake, Minnesota, 135, 136
Chinese festival, 161f.
Church of Sweden, 4
Clay, Henry, 102, 107
Clionian Society, 109
Coos Bay, 177

Delaware Swedes, 32
Democrats, 88, 108
Dietrichson, J. W. C., 17
Differentiation, 5
Dixon, Illinois, 154, 155n

East Union, Minnesota, 33
Easton, Pa., 119f.
Edstrom, Magnus, 150
Eielsen, Elling, 130, 130n
Eirich, Peter, 83
Ekman, A. J., 133
Engberg, Jonas, 155
Ersson, Anders, 55, 58, 65, 66
Ersson, Per, 60
Esbjörn, Lars P., 4, 6, 8, 14, 31, 65, 66, 66n, 67f., 70, 73, 76, 77, 87, 103, 131, 133, 139, 142, 143, 146, 147, 149, 154
Essick, A., 77, 77n, 83, 95, 100
Evangelical Lutheran Joint Synod of Ohio, 112, 141, 142, 143, 167
Ewing, Senator Thomas, 105
Exclusiveness, 6

Frid, S., 146

Gardiner, Robert H., 9
Galesburg, Illinois, 35, 66-68
Gefle, 49, 50
General Synod, 112, 141, 143n, 144, 147
Grabau, J. A. A., 125, 125n
Great Lakes, 11
Greeley, Horace, 105
Greenwald, Emmanuel, 94, 94n, 98, 101, 109, 111, 114, 116
Gustavus Adolphus College, 22, 34
Gustavus Adolphus congregation, 17

Häggström, Carl, 150
Hallgren, Jacob, 44
Hammarström, O., 56
Hamrin, O., 56
Harkey, Simon W., 144, 144n, 146, 147
Harm, Britta, 56
Hartzel, Abram, 72
Hassela, see Norrbäck
Hasselius, H., 66
Hasselquist, T. N., 17, 35, 131, 142, 146, 147, 154
Hatlestad, O. J., 146
Hauge, H. N., 130, 130n
Hedberg, F. G., 18, 24, 45n, 48n
Hedlund, Jonas, 44
Hedstrom, Jonas, 55f., 55n, 71

Hedstrom, Olof G., 6, 55, 55n, 124f., 147
Helsingland, 41, 48
Helsingör, 51
Henry, Patrick, 107
Hemlandet, 30, 34
Hoikka, Jacob, 160, 161, 163
Hokanson, M. F., 142, 154
Holm, Per, 131
Holm, Peter, 132 ff.
Home Mission Board, 23
Hudiksvall, 43, 44, 47, 49

Immigration and emigration, 1n, 2n
Inga Lotta (Mrs. E. Norelius), 146n

Jackson, Rev. Andrew, 26, 34
Janson, Eric, *see* Jannson, Eric
Janson, Olof, 65
Jansson, Eric, 60, 60n, 134n
Jansonites, *see* Eric Jansson
Jennische, Axel, 44
Johanson, Carl, 70-72
Johnson, Emeroy, 20n, 25n, 37
Johnson, William, 120
Joint Synod of Ohio, *see* Evangelical Lutheran Joint Synod
Jönsdotter, Lina, 41

Kamal, Hans, 65
King Charles XIV, 41
Kossuth, Louis, 92, 92n, 96f.

Larson, Anders, 65
LaSalle, Illinois, 12, 61, 66
Lehmann, W. F., 76, 76n, 93, 101, 114, 140

Lind, Jenny, 77, 77n, 87, 89
Lindblom, J. A., 43, 43n
Linder, F. O., 184-86
Lindh, L. O., 160, 161, 174, 197, 198, 199
Lindstrom, C. J., 133
Ludwig, Heinrich, 118, 120
Luther, Martin, 119, 119n
Lutheran Companion, 37
Lutheran Home Mission Society, 153
Lutheran Seminary, Springfield, Ill., 8
Lutheran Standard, 118, 118n, 119, 133

Marshalfield, 177f.
Mendota, Illinois, 154
Mix place, 66
Ministerial license, 142f.
Minnesota Elementar Läroverk, 33
Minnesota Lutheran Conference, 10n, 21, 25, 29, 30, 33, 34, 36
Minnesota Posten, 34
Minnesota Synod, 7, 26, 33
Minnesota Territory, 23, 27, 32
Mission Covenant Church, 17, 190n
Mississippi Conference, 144, 154n, *see also* United Scandinavian Conference
Mississippi Valley, 23
Mobeck, Frank, 133
Moline, Illinois, 69, 70, 130, 135, 138
Munter, M., 146

New Lutherans, 120, 120n

New York, 3, 4, 11, 17, 54
Nilson, Brita, 30
Nilson, Fredrik O., 138, 138n
Nilson, Olof, 65
Nilsson, John, 131, 148
Nilsson, Per, 148
Norberg, Captain, 54
Nord, Alfred, 54
Nord, Anders, 55, 65
Norelius, Andrew, 43, 48, 61, 62, 64, 66, 69, 90, 100, 107, 130
Norelius, Eric
  life in Sweden, 1f.
  arrival in America, 3f.
  ocean journey, 3
  national loyalty, 7n
  synodical president, 26
  new settler, 10f.
  churchman, 17f.
  humanitarian and educator, 26f.
  editor, 35n
  missionary, 156f.
Norelius, Jonas, 46
Norell, Jonas, 71
Norem, L. H., 146
Norrbäck, Hassela parish, 41, 42, 46

Ohio State Fair, 85f.
Olsson, John, 71
Öbom, A. G., 123

Palmquist, Gustaf, 7, 88, 88n, 103
Passavant, William A., 29, 33, 67, 67n, 70, 153, 168
Person, Jöns, 56
Person, Olof, 51
Persson, Andrew, 41

Pierce, Franklin, 106
Portland, Ore., 160
Princell, J. G., 17
Protestant Orphans Asylum, 30

Red Wing, Minnesota, 15, 23, 30, 33, 147, 148, 151, 200
Republican party, 34
Reynolds, Rev. William A., 67, 76, 77, 77n, 79, 82, 87, 98, 101, 107, 109, 111, 114, 116, 117, 140
Rix-dollar, 14, 45n, 48
Rock River Conference, see United Scandinavian Conference
Rock Island, Ill., 69
Rolin, Bäck and Lena, 71
Roman Catholic church, 82
Rosenius, C. O., 18, 19n, 23
Ryden, G. M., 177, 186, 199

St. Ansgar's Academy, 22, 34
St. Paul, Minnesota, 23, 27, 30, 133, 136, 200
Sandman, Eric, 82
San Francisco, 178f.
San Jose, 179ff.
Scandinavian Lutheran Synod, 8
Schmidt, H. I., 117
Schmucker, S. S., 143n, 147n
Schock, Rev. John, 119, 124
Schönberg, Olof, 43
Schwingle, Solomon, 83
Scott, Gen. Winfield, 105f.
Sioux Indian uprising, 28f.
Sjöblom, Peter, 26
Skandinavian, 123

Skans, J. W., 160, 164, 175, 192, 197, 199
Småland province, 123
Smith, Hans, 55, 61, 62, 63, 65, 69, 90
Smith, Dr. S. H., 78f.
Söderstrom, Peter, 71
Spring Garden, Minnesota, 150
Stanberg, Henry, 109
Stenholm, C. B., 146
Stohlmann, K. F. E., 124, 124n
Strand, Halvor, 33
Ström, Jonas, 71
Svedberg, Håkan, 131
Swedish Baptists, 138, 138n
Swedish Episcopalians, see Unonius, Gustaf
Swedish professorship, 89
Swensson, Jonas, 154
Synod of Northern Illinois, 8, 22, 131, 131n, 142, 143n, 144, 146, 155n

Telleen, John, 178, 179, 181, 185, 186, 199
Theummel, C. B., 146
Thomasson, Eric, 71
Tressler, J. A., 83, 83n
Turner, Frederick Jackson, 26

United Scandinavian Conference, 132n; see also Mississippi Conference, Chicago Conference
Unonius, Gustaf, 6, 21n, 59, 59n, 60

Valentine, C. J., 133
Värnstrom, C. G., 131
Vasa Children's Home, 30, 31
Vasa, Minnesota, 24, 30, 148

Wadlund, Anders, 62
Waldenstrom, P. P., 17
Waldenstrom controversy, 16, 17n
Wanberg, John, 150
Webster, Daniel, 107
Westerlund, Anders, 62-64
Westerlund, Eric, 53, 69
Whig political party, 88, 105, 108
Wiberg, Anders, 2, 7, 48, 103, 113f., 121
Wingård, Archbishop, 92
Workman, The, 168n
World Conference on Faith and Order, 9

Zethraeus, A. G., 143 f.

SEMINAR EDITIONS

Philip Jacob Spener, *Pia Desideria*. Translated, edited, and with an Introduction by Theodore G. Tappert.

Martin Kähler, *The So-Called Historical Jesus and the Historic, Biblical Christ*. Translated, edited, and with an Introduction by Carl E. Braaten.

Samuel Simon Schmucker, *Fraternal Appeal to the American Churches, with a Plan for Catholic Union on Apostolic Principles*. Edited and with an Introduction by Frederick K. Wentz.

Vilhelm Beck, *Memoirs*. A Story of Renewal in the Denmark of Kierkegaard and Grundtvig. Edited and with an Introduction by Paul C. Nyholm. Translated by C. A. Stub.

Nathan Söderblom, *The Nature of Revelation*. Edited and with an Introduction by Edgar M. Carlson. Translated by Frederic E. Pamp.

Eric Norelius, *The Journals of Eric Norelius: A Swedish Missionary on the American Frontier*. Translated, edited, and with an Introduction by G. Everett Arden.

Type: Body, 11 on 13 and 10 on 11 Garamond
Display, Garamond
Paper: 'R' Antique

2836